BRITANNIA IN BRIEF

BRITANNIA
in Brief
THE *SCOOP* ON ALL THINGS BRITISH

LESLIE BANKER *and* **WILLIAM MULLINS**

BALLANTINE BOOKS • NEW YORK

A Ballantine Books Trade Paperback Original

Copyright © 2009 by Leslie Banker and William Mullins

Published in the United States by Ballantine Books, an imprint
of The Random House Publishing Group, a division of Random
House, Inc., New York.

BALLANTINE and colophon are registered trademarks of
Random House, Inc.

Illustrations by Wesley Bedrosian

Grateful acknowledgment is made to Tate & Lyle for
permission to reprint "Lyle's Treacle Tart" from
Lyle's Golden Syrup website at www.lylesgoldensyrup.com.

LIBRARY OF CONGRESS CATALOGING-IN-PUBLICATION DATA
Banker, Leslie.
Britannia in brief: the scoop on all things British / Leslie
Banker and William Mullins.
p.   cm.
Includes index.
ISBN 978-0-345-50999-4
eBook ISBN 978-0-345-51290-1
1. Great Britain—Social life and customs—Miscellanea.
2. Great Britain—Description and travel—Miscellanea.
3. Great Britain—Civilization—Miscellanea.   4. National
characteristics, British—Miscellanea.   5. Popular culture—
Great Britain—Miscellanea.   I. Mullins, William.   II. Title.
DA589.4.B36 2009   941—dc22   2009008913

Printed in the United States of America

www.ballantinebooks.com

2 4 6 8 9 7 5 3 1

*Book design and map on page 3
by Simon M. Sullivan*

PREFACE

When we got engaged, we knew it was the dawn of an era of together-ness—living together, vacationing together, paying bills together, maybe even showering together—but writing a book together wasn't some-thing that we had ever considered. Then we spent a week in England visiting family, attending a friend's wedding, and going to a few dinner parties—it was the first time we'd been to the UK together—and Leslie, the native New Yorker, had about a million questions for William, the native Londoner. What's an "ASBO"? Who are "chavs," "yobs," and "hoodies"? How about a "TARDIS"? Who's more important, a duke or an earl? Is "bloody" a very bad word or a mildly bad word? What's "salad cream"? Is Kylie Minogue really an icon in the UK? Do I tip at a pub?

And what the heck is a "test match" at "Lord's"? Some of the questions were so basic they seemed embarrassing: Exactly what's the difference between the UK, Britain, and England? How often are parliamentary elections held? Is the UK a member of the EU? If so, then why do they use pounds instead of euros?

In short, over the course of that trip we realized the cultural divide between the US and the UK is really a gaping chasm. We needed a book that would answer all these questions once and for all. And so we wrote *Britannia in Brief*—together. And it worked out surprisingly well (except for a few minor nationality-based disagreements regarding punctuation and spelling).

Since we embarked on this project, we've been able to forgo the previously necessary debriefings on subsequent trips to the UK—whether they were about the Profumo Affair or Melvyn Bragg—and it was a huge relief for Leslie to finally get the jokes and join the conversation and for William to not have to answer so many questions.

We hope that you find as much satisfaction and enjoyment in reading *Britannia in Brief* as we had writing it (which is to say, it was a very positive experiment in togetherness).

CONTENTS

BRITANNIA IN BRIEF

CHAPTER 1

SO WHERE ARE WE ANYWAY?

*United Kingdom of Great Britain
and Northern Ireland*

ENGLAND? BRITAIN? UK? WHAT'S THE DIFFERENCE?

First things first: England, Great Britain, UK? All the same thing? These terms, which are so often used interchangeably, actually refer to distinct geographical and, frequently, political entities. Should you still think these distinctions are inconsequential after reading these pages, we invite you to visit, let's say, a bar in Scotland and inform the boys just how cute their English pub is. By the time your bruises and scars have healed, you will have had ample time to mull over the weightiness of these distinctions.

Scotland, England, and Wales are three separate nations all inhabiting the island of Britain.

What do we mean by "nation"? It is not our intention to burden you with medieval history and constitutional arcana, so suffice it to say, at one point Scotland and Wales were separate kingdoms, which at different points in time, and with varying degrees of resistance, fell sway to English rule through "Acts of Union." Lest you think this all sounds like a one-way transaction, it should be pointed out that such great "English" dynasties as the Stuarts and the Tudors had their roots in Scotland and Wales respectively.

The United Kingdom, or UK, is officially the United Kingdom of Great Britain (the big island) and Northern Ireland (the predominantly Protestant northeast quarter of the island of Ireland, distinct from the predominantly Catholic Republic of Ireland).

Broadly speaking, the inhabitants of the UK are called "the British" (and definitely not "the Uniteds" or "the Kingdoms"). So, while both a Welshman and a Scotsman are British, neither is English. Generally, though, people of the UK are more likely to describe themselves as Scottish, Welsh, Northern Irish, or English than as British. A Scotsman, by the way, is a Scot, and not Scotch, a term considered derogatory and best used only in America when ordering what in Scotland is simply called whisky (in the US spelled "whiskey").

We now offer you the exclusive "Peoples of the UK" Venn diagram:

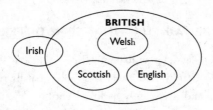

VITAL STATISTICS

Many of the cultural differences between the US and UK begin with
the basic fact that the UK is much smaller than the US.

UK Population in 2007: 60,975,000
US Population in 2007: 301,140,000
UK total land: 94,251 square miles (244,110 square kilometers,
smaller than Oregon)
US total land: 3,619,969 square miles (9,375,720 square kilometers)

GENERAL BRITISH FAQS

Is the UK a part of the European Union?
Yes, though you'd think it had been imposed at gunpoint by some
Franco-German mob to hear how people talk about it. Actually, in
1973 the British voted in a referendum and joined what was then
known as the European Economic Community. Conservatives argue
that the UK joined a free-trade zone that has become a superstate
where unelected bureaucrats in Brussels dictate what the British can
and cannot do. The more liberal argument is that after two world wars
ripped the continent apart in the last century, the EU has helped usher
in the longest period of peace in European history.

Then why doesn't the UK use the euro like other EU countries do?
Because the UK delayed joining the economic and monetary union
within the EU, and kept their own currency. There is still some lively
debate in the UK about whether they should trade their sterling for
euros. Another EU country that chose to forgo the euro is Denmark,
where in 2000 voters said "no" in a referendum to adopting the euro—
so the Danish krone is still used. It would be enormously difficult for
any British prime minister to commit the UK to joining the "eurozone"

without a referendum, and it is most likely that any vote on the matter would not favor giving up the pound.

What's the "Commonwealth"?

It's a group of independent states, primarily former colonies of Britain, that maintain an association of cooperation and recognize the reigning monarch of Britain as its symbol. Basically, it's what the British Empire has evolved, or devolved, into, depending on your point of view.

There are fifty-three independent states that are part of the Commonwealth, including Australia, the Bahamas, Bangladesh, Belize, Botswana, Canada, Cyprus, Ghana, India, Jamaica, Kenya, Malaysia, Maldives, New Zealand, Nigeria, Sierra Leone, Singapore, South Africa, Sri Lanka, Uganda, and, of course, the United Kingdom. Nations within the Commonwealth do not have ambassadors to one another; instead they exchange high commissioners.

What are the "Home Counties"?

These are the counties immediately around London. The counties of Kent, Surrey, Essex, Buckinghamshire, Berkshire, and Hertfordshire fall under the "Home Counties" umbrella, the smarter bits of which are sometimes referred to as the "stockbroker belt."

SNAPSHOTS OF BRITISH HISTORY

55 B.C.—Julius Caesar lands

Julius Caesar briefly lands in Kent but isn't too impressed. He came, he saw, he left.

A.D. 43—Roman occupation begins

The Roman emperor Claudius (of *I, Claudius* fame), in need of a political pick-me-up back home, invades England. England remains a part of the Roman Empire for almost four centuries, the last legions with-drawing early in the fifth century. Advantages: roads; peace; Italian food; founding of London, York, and other cities. Disadvantages: for-eign occupation; introduction of togas and other Roman items totally unsuited for wet, northern climates.

A.D. 61—Boudicca's rebellion

When a political opponent famously described Prime Minister Mar-garet Thatcher as "charging about like some bargain-basement Boadicea" during the Falklands War, they were comparing Thatcher with the orig-inal British warrior woman, Boudicca (known as Boadicea to the Ro-mans and the classically educated). Boudicca was the wife of an English client-king of the Romans. On his death, the Romans seized his king-dom, flogged Boudicca, and raped her daughters. Like some female Dirty Harry, she had her revenge, leading a vast and bloody rebellion against the Romans. However, as with Margaret Thatcher, her uncom-promising, take-no-prisoners approach eventually alienated all but her most committed supporters and led to her downfall.

In London, there is a famous statue of this national icon riding her war chariot by Westminster Bridge, next to Parliament Square.

Fifth Century A.D.

Angles, Saxons, Jutes, and other Germanic tribes pile over and fill the power vacuum in England created by the Romans' departure. Local na-tive Christians, like the semi-mythical King Arthur, try to fight them off but are ultimately subsumed by the invading WASPs (White Anglo-Saxon Pagans from northern Germany, in this case).

1066—Norman invasion

William "the Bastard" of Normandy lands in Sussex and defeats King Harold, who is killed by an arrow in the eye. William takes the crown and a new moniker: William "the Conqueror" (though he remains a complete bastard).

1215—Magna Carta

Under duress, a politically weakened King John grants "all freemen of our kingdom, for us and for our heirs forever" a series of rights and liberties detailed in the now-famous Magna Carta. This document established that no one, not even the sovereign, is above the law. The Habeas Corpus Act of 1679, which says that no freeman will be unfairly imprisoned, refers directly back to the Magna Carta as does the US Constitution, in particular the Bill of Rights.

1588—Spanish Armada

English sea captains are playing bowls in Plymouth when news arrives that a vast Spanish invasion fleet has been sighted. With a composure of which the nation is proud to this day, lead sea dog Sir Francis Drake insists they play on, "as there was plenty of time both to finish the game and beat the Spaniards after." Both of which they do, earning the defeat of the Spanish Armada recognition as perhaps England's greatest hour.

1640–60—English Civil War

This is a remarkably complicated and involved period in the island's history, and the bane of generations of British schoolchildren forced to study up on the Long, Rump, and Barebone's Parliaments, the Grand Remonstrance, and the Divine Right of Kings. In brief, Puritan forces—ideological brethren of those who came over to America on the *Mayflower* a couple of decades earlier—ride a general wave of discontent to overthrow and execute the high-handed Charles I, who, being a king, is a staunch believer in the Divine Right of Kings. Oliver Cromwell, the Puritan leader, refuses the crown but establishes himself as a virtual dictator. Today, he is largely remembered for his barbarity toward the Irish and the Puritans' priggish attempts to shutter the nation's theaters and ban Christmas festivities. By the time of Cromwell's death, people have come to miss the colorful if incompetent Stuarts, and King Charles I's son is invited back to reign as Charles II.

1688—Glorious Revolution of 1688

The so-called Glorious Revolution of 1688 might better be described as the Sneaky Dutch Invasion of 1688. Alarmed by the incompetence and incipient Catholicism of King James II, the king's opponents invite the staunchly Protestant Dutch prince William of Orange and his wife, Mary, who is King James's daughter, to come over and help themselves to the crown, which they promptly do. James flees to France but returns for a final showdown with his uppity son-in-law in Ireland. William's Protestant army trounces James's Catholic forces at the Battle of the Boyne, and the Protestants of Northern Ireland still celebrate the anniversary of the battle.

1745—Bonnie Prince Charlie and the last Scottish uprising

Simply referred to as "the Forty-five" in Scotland, the much mythologized uprising led by Charles Stuart, who is romantically remembered as "Bonnie Prince Charlie," is the last of many Scottish rebellions that attempted to restore the Scottish Stuarts to the British throne. The army of the likable but louche Charlie is thrashed by the English at Culloden Moor. After some months hiding out among the Highlanders, Charlie flees to France. The brutal English retribution pretty much puts an end to the traditional Highland way of life, requiring the Victorians to invent a romanticized past of clans and tartans a century later.

1940—Battle of Britain

The forecast for Britain in the summer of 1940 is severe: The Nazis occupy virtually the entire Atlantic seaboard of Europe; at the beginning of the summer a sizable portion of the British armory had been abandoned on the beaches of Dunkirk during the army's evacuation from France; both Russia and the US are still on the sidelines; and in May the weak and ineffective prime minister Neville Chamberlain had been forced to stand down, leaving a potential vacuum in the nation's leadership. From Adolf Hitler's viewpoint, the time is ripe for the invasion of England. The only thing he lacks is air superiority, and with that goal in mind he sends his air force, the Luftwaffe, to flush out and destroy Britain's Royal Air Force in the late summer of 1940.

Of course, no one embraces the role of underdog like the British, so Hitler is caught off guard by the determined response of the British people, their air force, and the grit of their new prime minister, Winston Churchill. The fierce air battles fought over southeast England pitch the RAF's Spitfires, flown by British, Polish, and Canadian pilots, against the Germans' Me 109s. In October, Hitler calls off the attack, realizing he can't sustain such heavy losses, and switches to the heavy bombing campaign now known as the Blitz.

1982—Falklands War

For a century and a half, Argentina had disputed Britain's claim to the Falkland Islands—a rocky outcrop of South Atlantic islands known to Argentines as Las Malvinas, with some two thousand residents, six hundred thousand sheep, and ten million penguins. In the spring of 1982, the crumbling military junta in Buenos Aires makes a desperate attempt to resuscitate their domestic popularity by invading the lightly defended Falklands and a handful of other British-owned rocks in the neighborhood. What the Argentine generals have not counted on is Margaret Thatcher, who wastes little time in dispatching a British fleet halfway around the world to counter the invasion. To the Conservatives in Britain, Thatcher is a tough patriot standing up for British sovereignty; to the left, she is a prime minister in need of a political boost herself who seizes an opportunity when she sees it.

The British fleet declares any Argentine vessel within two hundred miles of the islands will be sunk, and on May 2, 1982, a British submarine torpedoes the Argentine cruiser *General Belgrano,* which sinks, killing more than 320 sailors. That the ship was outside the exclusion zone is scarcely mentioned in the jingoistic British tabloids; *The Sun* leads with the now-famous headline "GOTCHA." Two days later, the Argentines score their biggest victory of the war, sinking the British destroyer HMS *Sheffield*. In late May, British ground forces attack and soundly defeat the largely underequipped and ill-trained Argentine conscripts in a number of battles across the islands.

On June 14, 1982, the Argentine general holding Port Stanley, the Falklands' capital, surrenders. In Argentina, the junta promptly resigns, paving the way for a return to a civilian-led democracy. In Britain, Margaret Thatcher and the Conservative Party ride the euphoria of victory to a near landslide in parliamentary elections a year later. The Argentine writer Jorge Luis Borges describes the war as being like "two bald men fighting over a comb."

July 7, 2005—The 7/7 bombings

During the morning rush hour in London on July 7, 2005, bombs explode on three underground trains and one bus. Approximately fifty-five people are killed and more than seven hundred are injured in a coordinated suicide bombing by Islamic militants. The explosions on the trains occur near Edgware Road station, Liverpool Street station, and between King's Cross and Russell Square stations. The bus explosion occurs at Tavistock Square. About two weeks later, there are four attempted bombings again on three trains and one bus—though this time the bombs never go off. The next day, an innocent Brazilian man is shot dead on a subway car by British police, who mistake him for a suspect from the attempted bombings the day before. Like the terrorist attacks of September 11, 2001, in the US, these bombings shake the nation.

THE PROUDEST MOMENTS IN BRITISH HISTORY

The defeat of the Spanish Armada, 1588 (see page 8).

British rule more than 25 percent of the earth's surface in 1921.

The Battle of Britain, 1940 (see page 9).

The Beatles occupy the top five spots on the *Billboard* Hot 100 in April 1964.

The 1966 World Cup (see page 82).

THE LEAST PROUD MOMENTS IN BRITISH HISTORY

Losing by penalties at any international football event.

Decline of the British Empire (ongoing).

January 30, 1972, "Bloody Sunday" (see page 15).

September 16, 1992, "Black Wednesday." The forced withdrawal of the sterling from the Exchange Rate Mechanism of the European Union as the pound plunged in value.

The knighting of Robert Mugabe, president of Zimbabwe, in 1994. (In 2008, the queen annulled his honorary knighthood.)

Release of *Spice World* (the Spice Girls' movie), 1997.

BITS AND PIECES OF PINK

Traditionally, pieces of the British Empire were colored pink on maps. This was a bit of a compromise: red was actually the color associated with the empire, but if the colonies, protectorates, mandates, and such were printed in red it was too difficult to read the place names within them. At its peak in the early 1920s, with the additions of the League of Nations–mandated territories in the Middle East, Africa, and the South Pacific, one-quarter of the globe was colored pink. It was the most extensive empire the world has ever seen. Nowadays, there's a lot less pink on the map, and though there are still a few outright colonies remaining, the word "empire" is not bandied about anymore. The queen does, however, remain the titular head of state of Canada and Australia, as well as of the independent states and dependent territories below.

Overseas Territories

Anguilla

Bermuda

British Indian Ocean Territory

British Virgin Islands

Cayman Islands

Falkland Islands

Gibraltar

Montserrat

Pitcairn Island

Saint Helena and dependencies,
  including Ascension Island and
  Tristan da Cunha

South Georgia

South Sandwich Islands

Turks and Caicos Islands

Independent States with British Monarch as Head of State

Antigua and Barbuda

Australia

The Bahamas

Barbados

Canada

Grenada

Jamaica

New Zealand

Papua New Guinea

Saint Kitts–Nevis

Saint Lucia

Saint Vincent and the Grenadines

Solomon Islands

Tuvalu

Crown Possessions

Channel Islands, including Jersey,
  Guernsey, Alderney, and
  Sark (in the English Channel)

Isle of Man (in the Irish Sea)

THE INS AND OUTS OF NORTHERN IRELAND

There are few subjects touchier than Northern Ireland. It appears that peace has finally come, and people who vowed never to shake hands are now shaking hands regularly and making some semblance of working together. Though former prime minister Tony Blair might be roundly criticized for sinking the UK into the morass of distant Iraq, he is nearly unanimously given credit for extracting the country from what had seemed like an endless quagmire closer to home. Hopefully "the Troubles" have finally ended.

The roots of the conflict stretch back eight hundred years to the first incursions into Ireland by the Norman rulers of England. Over the next few hundred years, the English used increasingly brutal methods to try to tame the unruly land. In the 1600s, colonists were shipped over, primarily from Scotland, to the northeastern Irish province of Ulster. It was hoped the stern Protestantism of these newcomers might drill some order into the place. That didn't happen, but the Protestants of Ulster made sure that when the rest of Ireland gained independence from England in 1921, their little corner stayed British. Hence, the Protestants are called "unionists" or "loyalists," the latter term having extremist connotations. The Protestant majority effectively disenfranchised the Catholic minority, leading to widespread disorder by the late 1960s when the British government sent in the army to reinforce the Protestant-dominated police force, the Royal Ulster Constabulary (RUC).

Loyalists = Hardline Protestants = Democratic Unionist Party (DUP)
Unionists = Moderate Protestants = Ulster Unionist Party (UUP)
Republicans = Hardline Catholics = Sinn Féin
Nationalist = Moderate Catholics = Social Democrat and Labour Party (SDLP)

The end of the 1960s also saw the start of the terrorist campaign by the Irish Republican Army (IRA), first in Northern Ireland and then in mainland Britain and beyond. About the same time, Protestant extremists formed their own terrorist gangs targeting Catholics in Northern Ireland. The British government clamped down, introducing direct rule from London, internment without trial, and, later, a ban on the broadcast of the voices of militant parties. All of which, combined with the British army's killing of thirteen unarmed Catholic protesters in Londonderry (the Protestants call it Londonderry, the Catholics call it Derry) on "Bloody Sunday" in 1972, led to an increase in political determination among both the militant republican and moderate nationalist factions of the Catholics.

The Good Friday Agreement of 1998 brought together the two sides, pressured by the US and British with bribes and threats. For that, the leaders of the two comparatively moderate parties, John Hume of the Catholic nationalist SDLP and David Trimble of the Protestant unionist UUP, split a Nobel Peace Prize. The Northern Irish voters, driven by deep mistrust, reacted a little differently, switching in droves to the extremist parties—the Catholics to Sinn Féin and the Protestants to the DUP. It wasn't until 2006 that all of the parties required for a workable peace sat down together.

From the Irish bars of Boston and New York, the struggle might have appeared as a valiant effort to liberate the last piece of Catholic Ireland from Protestant British occupation. Most everyone in the mainland UK, however, just wished they could do away with the place. But the British feel compelled to stay in Northern Ireland as long as the majority of the people there wish to remain a part of the United Kingdom, which they do (however unjust the past history that created that unionist majority).

Neither side in the conflict is viewed particularly sympathetically in mainland Britain. Particular dislike is reserved for the republicans, the anti-British Catholic extremist factions, whose long history of mainland and overseas terrorism is not easily forgiven. Since the Good Friday Agreement, both the republican and extremist Protestant loyalist militias have been adrift, carrying out the odd sectarian murder and drifting into criminal enterprises and irrelevance.

Emotions still run high, however, and it is better not to express any opinions on the matter of Northern Ireland unless explicitly asked. Those actually living in the province are trying to move on with their lives; those on the mainland are still angered by the memories of the bombing campaigns carried out by the IRA and would rather not talk about the centuries of barbaric conquest and oppressive occupation of

Ireland that got us to this point. All in all, it's better just to say that you hope things work out.

PEOPLE WHO ARE ...

FAMOUSLY NORTHERN IRISH
Gerry Adams
George Best
Kenneth Branagh
Seamus Heaney
Jameson Whiskey
Van Morrison

FAMOUSLY WELSH
Shirley Bassey
Richard Burton
Anthony Hopkins
Tom Jones
Dylan Thomas
Catherine Zeta-Jones

FAMOUSLY SCOTTISH
Gordon Brown
Robert the Bruce
Robert Burns
Sean Connery
Billy Connolly
Arthur Conan Doyle
Sheena Easton
Ewan MacGregor
Andy Murray
Robert Louis Stevenson
Rod Stewart

NICKNAMES

The Brits have a thing for nicknames. This includes nicknames of where people are from.

City	Nickname for Inhabitant	Proper Name for Inhabitant
Birmingham	Brummie	Birminghamian
Liverpool	Scouser	Liverpudlian
Newcastle	Geordie	Novocastrian
Manchester	Manc	Mancunian
Glasgow	Weegie	Glaswegian
Swansea	Jack	Swansean

TOWNS AND THEIR INDUSTRIES

Name	Industry
Aberdeen	Oil
Belfast	Shipping
Birmingham	Cars and candy
Cornwall	Tin
Glasgow	Shipping
Leicester	Lace
Newcastle	Shipping
Nottingham	Shoes
Sheffield	Steel and silver
Stoke-on-Trent	Pottery

SOME AMERICAN PLACES NAMED AFTER BRITS

Place	Named For
Baltimore, Maryland	Baron Baltimore of the Calvert family, the original proprietors of Maryland
Charleston, South Carolina	Named "Charles Town" in tribute to Charles II
Charlottesville, Virginia	George III's wife, Charlotte Sophia
Georgia	King George II
Jamestown, Rhode Island	James II, formerly the Duke of York
Jamestown, Virginia	James I (and VI, Scottishly speaking)
Maryland	Charles I's wife, Queen Henrietta Maria
New York	The Duke of York, later to become James II
North and South Carolina	Charles I and Charles II, from the Latin form of their name
Pittsburgh, Pennsylvania	British Prime Minister William Pitt the Elder
Virginia	Elizabeth I, the so-called Virgin Queen

MAJOR BRITISH RIVERS

River Avon (England)
River Bann (Northern Ireland)
River Clyde (Scotland)
River Dee (Scotland. There is also a river by this name in Wales
and England.)
River Exe (England)
River Forth (Scotland)
River Foyle (Northern Ireland)
River Humber (formed by the merging of the Ouse and Trent
rivers, England)
River Lagan (Northern Ireland)
River Mersey (England)
River Ouse (England)
River Severn (Wales and England)
River Tees (England)
River Thames (England)
River Trent (England)
River Tyne (England)

NEIGHBORHOODS OF LONDON

It takes only a brief amount of time spent outside the capital to realize
just how London-centric British government, media, and business are.
Love it or hate it, London dwarfs every other city in the country (its population is more than seven times the size of Birmingham, the next largest
city), and it is one of the richest, and most expensive, cities in the world.

POPULATIONS OF VARIOUS CITIES

New York City (2006)	8.25 million
Greater London (2007)	**7.56 million**
Los Angeles (2006)	3.85 million
Chicago (2006)	2.83 million
Houston (2006)	2.14 million
San Francisco (2006)	744,041
Washington, D.C. (2006)	581,530

At some point, almost all visitors to the UK find themselves in London. To the uninitiated it can seem bewildering: Why is it that when people refer to "The City," they're referring to the City of London and not London in general, and what's the difference? Greater London, which is approximately 660 square miles, comprises thirty-two boroughs, including the City of Westminster and the Royal Borough of Kensington and Chelsea, plus the aforementioned City of London. A broad look at the regions and selected neighborhoods of London follows.

THE CITY OF LONDON

Commonly referred to as "The City" or the "Square Mile," the City of London is one of the densest concentrations of banking and business in the world. Measuring a little over a square mile in size, The City stands on the site of the original Roman town of Londinium. Today it is a mix of ultramodern office buildings towering over centuries-old churches (there are about fifty churches in the Square Mile). Bustling with hundreds of thousands of workers during the day, The City is a ghost town at night, left to the nine thousand or so residents who actually live there.

THE WEST END

The heart of central London is the famous West End, home to theaters, shopping districts, office blocks, palaces, and museums. The West End is where London comes to work and play and visitors come to see the sights. It's home to such famous shopping destinations as Bond Street, Oxford Street, Covent Garden, Piccadilly, and Regent Street. Charing Cross, by Trafalgar Square, is considered the center of London and is the point from which distances from London are traditionally measured (to be exact, the site of the original Charing Cross is by the statue of King Charles I on the southern side of Trafalgar Square).

Piccadilly Circus and Leicester Square

This area is the Times Square of Great Britain, with all the bright lights, tacky gift shops, long-running musicals, and chain restaurants that implies. The Odeon Leicester Square cinema is where most of the big, splashy movie premieres unfurl, and Shaftesbury Avenue and Drury Lane are home to many of the famous West End theaters.

Soho

The original Soho, and the one neighborhood in London that never seems to sleep, Soho has been home to the city's sex industry for centuries. It also houses London's Chinatown and much of the film and music industry, and it is the hub of the capital's gay scene. Hundreds of cafés, pubs, restaurants, and bars give Soho a wonderful street life.

WEST LONDON

Home to the traditionally smart neighborhoods of Belgravia, Kensington, and Chelsea, as well as the long-standing West Indian community of Notting Hill and the ethnic melting pot of Shepherd's Bush, West London is big enough to include a lot of diversity. It stretches all the way from the West End out past Heathrow Airport to the west.

In centuries past, as London grew, the better-off neighborhoods were generally found on the western edge of development, where the prevailing west wind put them upwind of the stink of the increasingly crowded city. From this came the concentration of affluent neighborhoods to the west of the West End.

Chelsea

Chelsea is an elegant neighborhood, but don't come looking for excitement. The punks left the King's Road a long time ago and took with them any edginess the street had. The King's Road is now just another main street ("high street" as they say in Britain) of mostly chain stores. The Sloane Square end of King's Road has recently been given a facelift with the Duke of York Square development, a popular shopping destination with chic shops and cafés. The Peter Jones department store at Sloane Square, the bastion of sensible shopping for all Chelsea ladies, was also redone a few years ago, and there are plans afoot for a redevelopment of Sloane Square itself. Chelsea and South Kensington are both popular residential neighborhoods for American businesspeople living in London.

Knightsbridge and South Kensington

Home to the department stores Harrods and Harvey Nichols and an assortment of brightly lit boutiques, Knightsbridge is London's equivalent of New York's Fifth Avenue, chock-full of expensive shops and ladies who lunch. The area is a smart residential one, and though the main thoroughfares are perpetually traffic clogged, there are plenty of lovely side streets for shopping and strolling (Beauchamp Place and Walton Street are some of the most charming small shopping streets in London). Knightsbridge and South Kensington are characterized by garden squares packed behind broad boulevards.

Notting Hill

There was a time when Notting Hill was unquestionably the coolest place in London—this was the neighborhood that spawned and was lionized by the Clash, and it was here that Jimi Hendrix finally kissed the sky. That time is no longer. (How cool can a neighborhood really be when Julia Roberts and Hugh Grant have made an eponymous romantic comedy about it?) Today the area is one of the most expensive in London and home to such establishment figures as David Cameron, leader of the Conservative Party.

None of which is to denigrate the area. Notting Hill and the adjacent Ladbroke Grove are as fun as any neighborhood in London for a night out or a day's shopping. There are loads of great restaurants, cafés, and small boutiques, not to mention the hustle and bustle of the Portobello Market on the weekend. The area still maintains some of its traditional West Indian community whose annual Notting Hill Carnival on the August bank holiday weekend is a huge draw.

At the northern end of the neighborhood, Golborne Road is a fun mix of antique and fashion shops (with some big names like Stella McCartney), along with the restaurants of the Moroccan and Portuguese communities that predominate in this little patch.

NORTH LONDON

It is still easy to discern the villages that once made up North London before the city absorbed them. The patchwork of distinctive neighborhoods is what gives North London much of its charm, but also what makes it so confusing for London's other inhabitants to navigate. Hilly and high, Primrose Hill and Hampstead's Parliament Hill have the best vistas of London.

The area is famous for being the hub of London's liberal intelligentsia: Both Karl Marx and his coauthor Friedrich Engels lived in North London. So have such great British writers as William Blake, Samuel Taylor Coleridge, John Keats, and, in more recent years, Alan Bennett and Kingsley Amis. Intellectuals in residence have run the gamut from Sigmund Freud and Isaiah Berlin to Melvyn Bragg.

Camden Town

A little bit grungy, a little bit touristy, Camden has weathered hippies, punks, Goths, and armies of drunken Brits and Americans, all of which have made Camden the squabble of piercing shops, record stores, retro clothing stores, pubs, and music venues it is today. Camden Market, also called Camden Lock, is one of the great markets of London, along with Portobello and Spitalfields.

Hampstead

Formerly a bastion of the arts and intelligentsia, Hampstead now sports real estate prices that demand a banker's salary more than a poet's. One of the loveliest "villages" of London, Hampstead meanders on its medieval street layout and presents a complete hodgepodge of architectural styles. The rolling heath gives Hampstead a bucolic air.

Islington

Your opinions of Islington will probably depend on your opinions of well-off liberals. Love them and you'll find the bustling cafés and bistros of Upper Street delightful; loathe them and you'll probably retch at hearing another "Champagne socialist" discuss how fabulous the Harold Pinter play at the Almeida is. (The Nobel laureate premiered three of his plays at Islington's small, 325-seat Almeida Theatre.)

The area's strange juxtaposition of blocks of council flats (public housing) right next to streets of multimillion-dollar houses is characteristic of London, where the placing of postwar tower blocks (highrise apartment buildings) was dictated by the location of bomb sites as much as anything else.

Tony Blair lived in Islington before becoming prime minister. However, proving there are plenty of exceptions to all these generalizations, London's Conservative mayor Boris Johnson lives here as well.

Primrose Hill

You might never have been to Primrose Hill but you've seen it: The Rolling Stones, the Verve, Oasis, and Madness have all used it as a backdrop for record covers. Today the area has more than its share of rock stars; this is the smartest part of perpetually hip Camden, and who wouldn't love to have Regents Párk Road's bookstores, food shops, and restaurants on their doorstep?

THE EAST END

The traditionally working-class East End has been undergoing a renaissance of sorts lately. Broadly speaking, the area encompasses the neighborhoods to the east of the City of London and north of the River Thames. The areas around Spitalfields, Brick Lane, Shoreditch, and Hoxton Square have become the artistic center of the city, and the art dealers and restaurateurs who have arrived in the artists' wake have made the East End the new center of London cool, so much so that the new media types who dominate the area were subjects of a short-lived satirical sitcom, *Nathan Barley*. The area is home of the Hoxton Fin haircut—a term used to describe the sort of weekend Mohawk, known in America as the "faux-hawk," which can be comfortably patted down before heading to the office on Monday—considered illustrative of the new residents whose presence has driven prices in neighborhoods like Hoxton through the roof.

Over the centuries, the neighborhoods of the East End have been the entry point into Britain for successive waves of immigrants, from French Huguenots in the seventeenth century to East European Jews in the nineteenth century, followed by Bangladeshis and then Somalians in recent years. Starting in the 1980s with the commercial and residential Canary Wharf development on the Isle of Dogs and continuing with construction for the 2012 Summer Olympics, which will be centered in east London, the area has been making up for decades of underinvestment.

Shoreditch and Hoxton

The center of the new East End scene, Shoreditch and Hoxton are great for a night out, with galleries, restaurants, and scenester clubs like Shoreditch House (sister club to the Soho Houses in London, New York, and Los Angeles), though there is also a surplus of self-regarding hipsters. For those whose tastes don't run to the bleeding-edge art on display in the ubiquitous galleries, there are still plenty of seedy old strip clubs around.

Spitalfields and Brick Lane

Though the office blocks of the neighboring City of London are beginning to creep into Spitalfields, the area encompassing Old Spitalfields Market, Hawksmoor's stunning Christ Church, and Brick Lane still contains a great mix of trendy art, ethnic flavors, and old-school Cockney style. Brick Lane is the center of London's Bangladeshi community—the street signs are even bilingual—and is a must for anyone with a taste for curry. There's also a large market on Sundays. At the end of Brick Lane is the Whitechapel Art Gallery, the contemporary art museum that can probably take much of the credit for making this and the adjoining neighborhoods such an artistic hotbed.

SOUTH LONDON

South London has long labored under the bias of being on the wrong side of the river. Vast and sprawling, many of the neighborhoods south of the Thames are faceless dormitory communities, yet among them, particularly closer to the river, are some the loveliest and liveliest parts of London. There is a long and only semi-friendly rivalry between North and South London.

Brixton

The heart of the West Indies, but with English weather. Check out the market on Electric Avenue (made famous in the Eddy Grant song of the 1980s) to see a slightly overly authentic Caribbean and African food market. ("What part of a goat did you say that was?") There's a big clubbing and live music scene at night, but keep your wits about you if you go: Brixton is well known for its gangs of "Yardies" and street violence.

Clapham and Battersea

Jokingly belittled as "South Chelsea," Battersea aspires to the chic of the real Chelsea just across the river. So close and yet so far. Clapham was once held to be the archetypal anonymous suburb—you'll still hear the English Everyman referred to as "the man on the Clapham omnibus"—though it has now, along with neighboring Balham and Wandsworth, become the place to live for professionals with families who have been priced out of West London. Here in the "Nappy Valley" they can purchase Victorian terrace houses with hallways big enough for strollers, take walks with their children and dogs on the expanse of Clapham Common, and still be only fifteen minutes by train from The City.

GEOGRAPHICAL ANALOGIES

Shaftesbury Avenue, London	=	Broadway, New York
Leicester Square and Piccadilly Circus, London	=	Times Square, New York
Guildford, England	=	Fairfield County, Connecticut
Brighton	=	San Francisco, California
Slough	=	White Plains, New York
Essex	=	New Jersey
Cornwall	=	Coastal Maine
The Cotswolds	=	The Berkshires
North Wales	=	Canada
South Wales	=	The Rust Belt
Birmingham	=	Detroit, Michigan
Bournville (near Birmingham, home of Cadburys)	=	Hershey, Pennsylvania

Sheffield	=	Pittsburgh, Pennsylvania
The Lake District	=	The Adirondacks
The Scottish Highlands	=	The Wild West
Africa	=	Guatemala*
Benidorm, Spain	=	Panama City Beach, Florida
		(party central)
Los Angeles	=	Los Angeles

* where people from the UK and US respectively go to do charity work and feel better about themselves.

FACT OR FICTION?

The British are eternally grateful to the US for their help during World War II.
Fiction. "Overpaid, oversexed, and over here" was the catchphrase repeated around Britain about the American soldiers stationed there during WWII. It might come as a surprise, but the British did not relish every moment that the Americans were on their soil helping to win "The War."

The Isle of Man is a tax haven for wealthy residents.
Fact. Like in Monaco and other tax refuges, people with money don't have to pay lots of taxes if they live on the Isle of Man. But the Isle of Man is up in the Irish Sea with an average August temperature of 58°F, whereas a place like Monaco has the sunny beaches of the Mediterranean going for it. Other local tax havens include Guernsey and Jersey in the Channel Islands off the coast of France.

Scottish people have a reputation for spending lavish amounts of money on luxuries.
Fiction. It's a broad generalization, but Scottish people have a reputation for being very thrifty.

The Welsh are famous for their dancing and fast-paced hand clapping.
Fiction. The Welsh are renowned for their singing—not so much dancing and hand clapping. The nation has a centuries-long tradition of song, stretching from their ancient bards to Tom Jones, Shirley Bassey, and the Manic Street Preachers.

Liverpool is home to many comedians.
Fact. Liverpool has long been famous for producing generations of Britain's top comedians. Though not familiar to American audiences, Liverpudlian comedians Arthur Askey, Ken Dodd, Les Dennis, Jimmy Tarbuck, and Alexei Sayle, to name a few, are household names in the UK. Liverpool's also traditionally done very well in producing football players and pop stars, including that rather well-known skiffle combo, the Beatles.

Brighton is a newly gentrified neighborhood in East London.
Fiction. Brighton, though technically not a neighborhood of London (it's actually about sixty miles away), has become a London-by-the-Sea where house prices can be the same as in the city. It's very stylish, with beautiful beaches, little lanes, and commuters lining up to take the train up to London for work.

CHAPTER 2

SOCIETY

THE CLASS SYSTEM

Perhaps nothing about the British intrigues and confounds Americans quite as much as the class system. Americans can take comfort in the fact that the British themselves are equally intrigued and confounded by it. For the foreigner, class is a topic best not broached in conversation. You are liable to unwittingly step on toes and give offense, however pure your intentions might be. And, as to your own place in the social firmament, don't fret over it; your very foreignness puts you outside the realms of classification. Basically, the topic of social class is a big thorny hairball that's best left to the experts.

The British embrace their social position to a degree not seen in the more aspirational US. When asked to define their social class, polls in

2006 and 2007 showed that a solid 90 percent of Americans define themselves as middle-class (instead of "upper-class" or "lower-class"), which is telling in a country where more than 12 percent live below the poverty line. In Britain, well over half of the population defines themselves as working-class. One 2002 poll showed that 68 percent of the population agreed with the statement: "At the end of the day, I'm working-class and proud of it." Just because they're proudly working-class doesn't mean they're poor, though; there's plenty of opportunity for socioeconomic mobility in today's Britain. It's just that people carry their class with them as they move up and down the economic ladder.

Visitors often seem baffled by the British ability to discern a fellow Brit's background and social status within seconds. Those who think of this as some anachronistic sixth sense are not entirely mistaken. Though many things give away a person's origin, accent indicates it more than anything else, and the British ear is unconsciously trained from birth to pick up on the subtlest indicators of geography, education, and upbringing. The Irish playwright George Bernard Shaw, in his play *Pygmalion,* summed up the antagonism this engenders when Henry Higgins said, "It is impossible for an Englishman to open his mouth without making some other Englishman hate or despise him."

Americans may be taken aback by how matter-of-factly a British person pegs someone as middle-class, working-class, or upper-class. In the US, class is not such an obvious or overtly stated label, and terms such as "white collar" and "blue collar" are often used instead.

TITLES AND HONORS

Modern Britain is one of the last countries in the world with a full-on, government-sanctioned titled aristocracy. Sure, every other Italian man you meet might style himself a prince, but no one knows who's for real and who's a fake. Though the British titled classes no longer hold much political power, they still hold great social clout and fascinate Americans to a degree that other legitimate government-recognized aristocracies, such as those of Spain and Sweden, just can't match.

Traditionally, kings and queens bestowed titles on their political fixers, generals, and such pillars of the establishment as their illegitimate children and drinking buddies. While today the monarch still personally awards some honors and titles, by and large they are on the "recommendation" of the prime minister, who awards them for political service or public achievement.

The British love making fun of Americans who buy purported feudal titles that supposedly permit their owners to style themselves "Lord of the Manor," as though real titles haven't been bought and sold just as brazenly over the years to the social climbing and ambitious British. Prime minister David Lloyd George put price tags on knighthoods, baronetcies, and peerages in the years following World War I; prime minister Harold Wilson elevated some rather unsuitable friends of his to the peerage in the 1970s with his so-called Lavender List; and Tony Blair's government underwent an embarrassing police investigation after revelations that a number of those he had proposed for peerages had made large, undeclared loans to his Labour Party. The power to grant peerages is a honey pot that prime ministers have a hard time keeping their paws out of.

So-called peers have titles ranging from duke and duchess to baron and baroness, and they traditionally held seats in the House of Lords. A "hereditary peer" inherits his title from his father, whereas a "life peer" is given a title and has it only for as long as he or she is alive. Recently, hereditary peers have been almost entirely turfed out of the House of Lords, and seats are held primarily by life peers. Further reforms could change this in the near future. Historically, the title of "baron" was hereditary, passing from father to eldest son. In 1958, this was changed so that all barons and baronesses created from that date forward would hold the title only for life. Barons and baronesses given their titles before 1958 remain hereditary. Ranks of the peerage above baron remain hereditary, as well, though it is very rare that a new earl, viscount, or duke is minted. On the occasion when someone is ennobled as a hereditary peer nowadays, it tends to be someone unlikely to produce an heir, as was the case when Maggie Thatcher had Home Secretary Willie Whitelaw created viscount in 1983 at age sixty-three.

Telling of their feudal origin, peerages are associated with a place. On elevation to the peerage, you get to choose a place with which you have an association, as long as it's not already taken by another peer. This produces such wonderful titles as that of the life peer Baroness Gardener of Parkes.

Titles in Britain follow a strict precedence, and though no one is expected to remember all the intricate details, it's helpful to have some idea of the relative weightiness of the different titles. We present the following list, so you'll at least know who trumps whom. From most important to least important:

The monarch. The king or queen trumps all.

Royal duke and duchess. These are titles within the monarch's family, such as the Duke of York.

Duke and duchess. Non-royal dukes, such as the Duke of Westminster.

Marquess, pronounced "maar-kee," and **marchioness,** "marsha-ness."

Earl and countess. If a duke, marquess, or earl has multiple titles, as is common, his eldest son may style himself with one of the lesser ones as a "courtesy title." Courtesy titles, however, don't trump actual titles.

Viscount ("vye-count") and **viscountess** ("vye-count-ess"). In the European hierarchy, this title tended to fall to a count's younger brother or son. In the British system, it is its own distinct rank, as Britain has no rank of count.

Baron and baroness. These are your standard-issue lords and ladies and are the lowest ranks in the peerage, that is, the lowest ranks traditionally found in the House of Lords.

Baronetcy. Though the title is hereditary, baronets are not part of the peerage. The seniority of a baronetcy is determined by the date it was created. There are a tiny handful of Scottish baronetcies that can descend down the female line.

Knights. When you hear about Sir Such-and-Such, more often than not that person is a knight (otherwise he's a baronet). A female knight is a dame.

The rest of us hoi polloi.

The following is a quick guide to the usage of these titles. Here we chart the rise of Posh and Becks through the ranks of the aristocracy.

Rank	Spoken Style	Spouse's Spoken Style	Envelope Style
Duke	Duke (or Your Grace)	Duchess (or Your Grace)	His Grace the Duke of Los Angeles
Marquess	Lord Beckham	Lady Beckham	The Most Hon. the Marquess of Los Angeles
Earl	Lord Beckham	Lady Beckham	The Rt. Hon. the Earl of Los Angeles
Viscount	Lord Beckham	Lady Beckham	The Rt. Hon. the Viscount Beckham

Rank	Spoken Style	Spouse's Spoken Style	Envelope Style
Baron	Lord Beckham	Lady Beckham	The Rt. Hon. the Lord Beckham
Baroness	Lady Beckham	Mr. Beckham	The Rt. Hon. the Baroness Beckham
Child of a Baron or Baroness	Mr. Beckham	Mrs. Beckham	The Hon. Brooklyn Beckham
Baronet	Sir David	Lady Beckham	Sir David Beckham, Bt.
Knight	Sir David	Lady Beckham	Sir David Beckham
Dame	Dame Victoria	Mr. Beckham	Dame Victoria Beckham

Journalists, American and British alike, sometimes make the mistake of referring to a peer as Lord Joe Smith, using his full name. This is incorrect; a peer is simply Lord Smith. When someone is styled as Lord or Lady using the full name, it's typically a courtesy title for the younger sons of a duke or marquess or the daughters of a duke, marquess, or earl. For example, Lady Diana Spencer was the daughter of Earl Spencer. Her mother, while her parents were married, would have been Lady Spencer. While a courtesy title counts for something, it's not like holding the actual title.

ON BEING KNIGHTED

The monarch, or the monarch's representative, knights a kneeling subject by touching him on the shoulders with the tip of a sword and pronouncing the magic words "Arise Sir . . ." This is called "dubbing." For dames and clergymen, the monarch skips the sword.

There are various orders of knighthood, such as the Knights of the Garter, the Order of the Bath, and the Order of St. Michael and St. George, which come with their own pecking order. These distinctions are lost on most of us, but in certain circles they carry great weight.

Members of the civil service rise through the ranks of the Order of St. Michael and St. George from companion (CMG), to knight commander (KCMG), to grand cross (GCMG), the initials for which are jokingly said to stand for, respectively, "Call Me God," "Kindly Call Me God," and, ultimately, "God Calls Me God."

Those who are not British but have made an important contribution to British interests can receive an honorary knighthood. Recipients of this have included Microsoft's Bill Gates, ex–New York mayor Rudy Giuliani, and film director Steven Spielberg. The recipients of an honorary knighthood may not call themselves "sir" or "dame," though they are permitted to use the initials, such as KBE (for "Knight of the British Empire"), after their names.

OTHER HONORS (OR RATHER, HONOURS)

You will sometimes see letters such as CBE, OBE, or MBE after a person's name. These are honors below the rank of knight that are bestowed upon a person by the monarch for merit, service, or bravery. There is a strict order of precedence and a great variety of honors. The ones above are listed in order of importance from top to bottom and stand for:

CBE = Commander of the Order of the British Empire
OBE = Officer of Order of British Empire
MBE = Member of Order of British Empire

Keeping titles straight and properly addressing people with titles is complicated business. The final word on how to get it right is the book *Debrett's Correct Form*.

PROPER PROTOCOL WHEN YOU MEET THE MONARCH

If you are invited to meet the reigning monarch of Britain, keep in mind the following to avoid committing grievous faux pas that could haunt you for years to come.

- Stand when the king or queen enters the room. Men should bow from the head, not a full waist bow, and women should curtsey.
- The first time you reference the monarch say, "Your Majesty" or "Your Royal Highness." From then on you can address her as "ma'am" or, in the case of a king, as "sir."
- If you ask about a member of their family, use the person's full title. It would be inappropriate to ask, "How is your son Edward?"
- Don't say "Pleased to meet you," because of course you are pleased to meet the monarch.
- Don't turn your back on the monarch.
- High-fiving, winking, chewing gum, showing off your tattoos, and big bear hugs are inappropriate.

ROYAL FAQS

Who are Brenda and Phil the Greek?

They are none other than Queen Elizabeth II and her husband, Prince Philip, Duke of Edinburgh. The satirical current affairs magazine *Private Eye* made up the nicknames as a running joke. Prince Philip, though he isn't actually Greek, is a member of the Greek royal family, which is famous for being not very Greek at all. (His father was Prince Andrew of Greece, though his ancestry was just about all northern European.) As for Brenda, *Private Eye,* which is known for its inside jokes, gave all of the royal family lower-class, not-very-royal-sounding nicknames, including Brian for Prince Charles, Cheryl for Princess Diana, and Keith, another name for Prince Philip.

Everyone seems to have loved the Queen Mum. Why is that?

The Queen Mum, aka Her Majesty Queen Elizabeth, the Queen Mother, was a particularly beloved member of the royal family. Lady Elizabeth Bowes-Lyon, who was Scottish, was born in 1900. In 1923, she married Prince Albert, Duke of York, the second son of King George V.

Prince Albert unexpectedly became King George VI in 1936 when his older brother, King Edward VIII, abdicated the throne to marry the American divorcée Wallis Simpson. While her husband was famously shy, the queen consort of King George VI (as she was then known) played an active role in supporting the monarchy and repairing its battered image after the scandal surrounding Edward VIII's abdication.

What made her particularly popular was her refusal to leave London during German bombing raids in World War II. She was an active presence in the city during this time and famous for saying, after Buckingham Palace was bombed, "I'm glad we've been bombed. It makes me feel I can look the East End [the poor, working-class section of London, which was hammered by German bombing] in the eye." When King George VI died in 1952, their daughter Elizabeth ascended to the throne. The Queen Mum, who was rumored to have a penchant for gin, remained active in her royal duties until her death in 2002.

Don't forget: The royals that keep their mouths shut are more popular than those who have opinions.

Why does the monarch have two birthdays?

Since Edward VII's reign the monarch has had an official birthday held during the summer months when the weather is warm and the time is best for a public celebration. Additionally, there is his or her real birthday. Queen Elizabeth II was born on April 21, 1926, though she celebrates her official birthday on a Saturday in June.

How do you know when the monarch is in residence?

The royal standard is flown when the monarch is in residence. The Union Flag is flown when the monarch is not in residence. The Union

Flag, commonly called the Union Jack, is the British flag that we are familiar with: It has a red cross outlined in white, a secondary red cross behind the primary one, and a deep blue background. The royal standard is a totally different flag. It is divided into quadrants. The top left and lower right each have three golden lions on a red background, which represent England; the upper right quadrant shows a red lion on a gold field, which represents Scotland; and the lower left quadrant has a golden harp on a blue background, which represents Ireland. In Scotland, a slightly different royal standard flies. Its upper left and lower right quadrants have the red lion and gold background that represents Scotland, and the upper right quadrant shows the three golden lions that represent England.

A NOTE ON THE UNION FLAG

The flag of the United Kingdom is commonly called the Union Jack and officially called the Union Flag. It's a combination of the Cross of Saint George (England), the Cross of Saint Patrick (Ireland), and the Cross of Saint Andrew (Scotland). Wales isn't represented on the flag because when the first version of the flag appeared Wales was already united with England.

In the UK, it's much less common to see the Union Flag flying in front of the average person's house or in front of stores the way the Stars and Stripes are flown in the US, in part due to the flag's hijacking by the extreme right wing.

THE ROYAL RESIDENCES

Buckingham Palace, in the borough of Westminster in London, was built in 1705 for John Sheffield, Duke of Buckingham, and, after some expanding and renovating, became the London residence of Britain's sovereign in

1837 when Queen Victoria moved in. Buckingham Palace has the popular Changing of the Guard, the Queen's Gallery at Buckingham Palace with rotating exhibitions from the royal collection, and the Royal Mews, where visitors can see the carriages kept for royal processions.

Kensington Palace is also located in London, on the west side of Kensington Gardens. It was the residence of the reigning monarch from 1689 until 1760. Queen Victoria was born at Kensington Palace and lived there until she ascended to the throne in 1837, at which point she moved to Buckingham Palace. Princess Diana lived in Kensington Palace after her divorce from Prince Charles, and flowers are still left outside the gates in her memory. Other members of the royal family live there today in what are called grace-and-favor residences. Sections of the building are open to the public.

Saint James's Palace is still the official residence of the monarch, though since Queen Victoria decamped to the nearby Buckingham Palace in 1837, none has actually lived there. It is in acknowledgment of this status that foreign ambassadors to Britain are still accredited "to the Court of St. James's." Though Princess Anne and Princess Alexandra both have apartments there, the bulk of the palace is given over to reception rooms, the monarch's administrative offices, and the private offices of certain royals, including Princes William and Harry.

Clarence House was built next to Saint James's Palace in the 1820s for Prince William Henry, Duke of Clarence, who stayed there once he became King William IV in 1830. Other royal occupants have included Queen Elizabeth II and Prince Philip, who lived there after they married in 1947 until she ascended to the throne in 1952. At that point Queen Elizabeth swapped with her mother, the Queen Mum, who lived in Clarence House until her death in 2002. Clarence House is now the official London residence of the Prince of Wales (aka Charles) and the Duchess of Cornwall (aka Camilla Parker-Bowles) as well as Princes Harry and William. It is open to the public during the summer.

Windsor Castle has been a residence of monarchs for about nine hundred years. It's approximately twenty-five miles from London and is the largest occupied castle in the world. Damaged by a fire in 1992, it has been restored and is open to the public, though some sections are closed when the royal family is in residence, typically in the spring and December. Public outrage at the government-funded expense of refurbishment after the fire compelled the queen to start paying taxes.

Frogmore House is a relatively small country house on the property of Windsor Castle. It has been used as a country house by monarchs since the seventeenth century. Queen Victoria and Prince Albert are buried in the garden there; it was a favorite place of hers. It is open to the public for tours.

The Palace of Holyroodhouse in Edinburgh, is the official residence of the monarch in Scotland. Mary, Queen of Scots, lived in the palace from 1561 to 1567. It was also the headquarters of Bonnie Prince Charlie during the infamous 1745 uprising. The queen currently spends some time there for official functions. It is open to the public.

Balmoral Castle is on the River Dee in Aberdeenshire, Scotland. Purchased by Queen Victoria's husband, Prince Albert, it is a privately managed working estate, not an official residence. Queen Elizabeth II typically spends the late summer there. Sitting on about fifty thousand acres, it is open to the public for tours from April through July and has holiday cottages that can be rented.

Sandringham House in Norfolk has been the private house of British sovereigns since 1862. Like Balmoral Castle, it's a working estate that is managed privately. The royal family often spends Christmas and January there, though it's open to the public for tours from Easter until October.

TRICK QUESTION: WHO MARRIED UP, CHARLES OR DIANA?

In matters of sheer physical height, it was a draw; Charles and Diana were both about five foot ten or eleven. (Charles stood on a box for the official portraits of the young couple, making him appear almost a head taller. The royal family is famously diminutive.) In matters of class, however, the snobs of England see a clear winner, and it's not who you might presume.

Though you'll never hear it said, the aristocracy have never quite gotten used to the fact that the royal family are, well, German. In certain quarters, people remember that it was only during World War I that the family was rebranded "Windsor" from "Saxe-Coburg-Gotha" in response to strong anti-German sentiment. In contrast, Diana's family, the Spencers, are scions of some of the grandest English nobility.

THE WIT AND WISDOM OF PRINCE PHILIP

Queen Elizabeth's husband, Prince Philip, is well known for his gaffes. Tasteless? Quite possibly. Inconsiderate? Most certainly. And yet, there is sometimes a strange wisdom to his musings.

- He asked a driving instructor in Oban, Scotland: "How do you keep the natives off the booze long enough to pass the test?"
- To a blind woman with a guide dog: "Do you know they have eating dogs for the anorexic now?"
- During the 1981 recession: "Everybody was saying we must have more leisure. Now they are complaining they are unemployed."
- To a group of deaf children standing next to a Jamaican steel drum band, on his visit to the new National Assembly for Wales: "Deaf? If you are near there, no wonder you are deaf."
- "When a man opens a car door for his wife, it's either a new car or a new wife."
- To the queen, after her coronation: "Where did you get that hat?"

BRITISH DYNASTIES

The current royal family, the Windsors, haven't always ruled Britain. Over the centuries, a number of different families of different nationalities and backgrounds have occupied the throne. For the past few hundred years, the shifting of dynasties has been surprisingly peaceful, with transitions taking place through marriage or inheritance. Needless to say, there were more than enough violent seizures of the crown in the past to compensate for the stability of recent centuries.

THE NORMANS

Every schoolchild in Britain knows what happened in 1066: William the Conqueror and his Normans invaded England from Normandy in France and defeated the Saxons under King Harold at the Battle of Hastings. From there it all gets a bit hazy. The Norman dynasty lasted for three generations until 1154: Two of William the Conqueror's sons ruled competently before things devolved into a lengthy and complicated civil war between two of his grandchildren.

THE PLANTAGENETS

A remarkably long-lasting dynasty, given to frequent fratricidal civil wars and plots, the Plantagenets gave England fourteen monarchs between 1154 and 1485. In fact, the Plantagenets are often broken down as four separate branches of the dynasty—Angevins, Plantagenets, Lancastrians, and Yorkists. The seventeenth-century essayist Francis Bacon described them as "a race often dipped in their own blood," yet among their number were such name-brand monarchs as Richard the Lion-Hearted; bad King John, persecutor of Robin Hood; Edward I, conqueror of Ireland; and Henry V, of Shakespeare fame.

THE TUDORS

Short-lived but chock-full of famous names, the Tudors reigned for little more than a century—from Henry VII (1485–1509), who gained the throne after winning a series of civil wars, collectively known as the Wars of the Roses, through Elizabeth I (1558–1603).

Henry VII (1485–1509)
His reign brought a welcome end to years of civil war.

Henry VIII (1509–47)
Famous for his six wives and for founding the Church of England (the two achievements not being unrelated).

▭▭▭ *A Man for All Seasons* (1966)

Edward VI (1547–53)
Sickly son of Henry VIII; died at sixteen.

▭▭▭ *The Prince and the Pauper* (various)

Mary I (1553–58)
Daughter of Henry VIII; nicknamed "Bloody Mary" for the zeal with which she persecuted Protestants in her futile attempt to return England to the Roman Catholic Church.

Elizabeth I (1558–1603)
Another daughter of Henry VIII; known for whipping the Spanish Armada and beginning the colonization of America. She famously never married.

▭▭▭ *Elizabeth* (1998); *Elizabeth: The Golden Age* (2007)

▭▭▭ Denotes a movie about the monarch

📺 Denotes a television show about the monarch

THE STUARTS

While the Tudors ruled England and Wales, the still independent Scotland was governed by the Stuarts, who had ruled there since 1371. When Elizabeth I of England died childless, the crown defaulted to her closest male heir, who happened to be her cousin, James VI of Scotland. There was a certain irony in James inheriting the throne of the woman who had executed his own mother, Mary, Queen of Scots.

James I (1603–25; king of Scotland 1567–1625)

Called "James VI and I" in Scotland, he brought the whole island of Britain together under one crown (though it would be another century before the Act of Union brought them together politically). James famously hated the newfangled tobacco craze then sweeping the nation.

 Blackadder: The Cavalier Years (1988, BBC TV)

Charles I (1625–49)

His high-handedness instigated a civil war, which he lost, along with his head.

Interregnum: The English Civil War and the rule of Oliver Cromwell (see page 8).

Charles II (1660–85)

Fairly useless son of Charles I, invited to resume the dynasty after the death of Oliver Cromwell. The actress and libertine Nell Gwyn was his mistress.

Restoration (1995)

James II (1685–88)

Utterly useless younger son of Charles I. He was bumped by his daughter Mary and her Dutch husband, William (who also happened to be James II's nephew). He lived out his days in France (see page 9).

William III (1689–1702) and Mary II (1689–94)

Joint rulers. They had the architect Sir Christopher Wren fix up the then suburban Kensington Palace as their London residence since the city aggravated William's asthma, and his inability to speak English aggravated his subjects. The College of William and Mary in Virginia, the second oldest university in the US, is named after them.

Anne (1702–14)

Daughter of James II and namesake of the Queen Anne style of architecture and design. She outlived all seventeen of her children and so ended the Stuart dynasty, though not for want of trying to produce an heir.

THE HANOVERIANS

On Queen Anne's death, the crown passed to her distant cousin Georg Ludwig, prince of Hanover in Germany, who was rebranded with the more English name George I. Ruling for almost two hundred years—from 1714 until 1901—the house of Hanover is the longest reigning dynasty after the medieval Plantagenets. Nearly every Hanoverian monarch, from George I through Victoria, seems to have had a terrible relationship with his or her heir.

George I (1714–27)

Never bothered to learn English and spent as little time in Britain as he could, preferring to stay home in Germany. Being abroad most of the time, George delegated power to Robert Walpole, who became Britain's first prime minister. George's philosophy and shaky command of the English language is summed up in his pronouncement: "I hate all boets and bainters." (He wasn't a complete philistine though: He was patron to the composer Handel.)

George II (1727–60)

Like his father, George II preferred to spend his time in Germany. He was the last British monarch to personally lead an army into battle.

George III (1760–1820)

Famously lost his American colonies and later went mad. His periodic bouts of insanity are conjectured to be have been caused by the rare metabolic disease porphyria.

🎬 *The Madness of King George* (1994)

George IV (1820–30)

Ran the country for the last decade of his father's life. The younger George was thoroughly extravagant and debauched and not very popular. His secret marriage to the Catholic Maria Fitzherbert was notorious.

William IV (1830–37)

Younger brother of George IV. He was, by all accounts, a very charming, if not particularly talented, man. He left no (legitimate) children, and so the crown went to his eighteen-year-old niece, Victoria.

Victoria I (1837–1901; empress of India from 1876)

Longest reigning monarch in British history. The British Empire was at its zenith of power during Victoria's tenure: This was the Victorian age.

🎬 *Mrs. Brown* (1997)

THE SAXE-COBURG-GOTHAS

When Victoria's son came to the throne as Edward VII, he took his father's surname, Saxe-Coburg-Gotha. While it might seem a bit much to call this a new dynasty—there was, after all, no break in the line—those who officiate on such things declare it so. One shouldn't worry unduly about it, as Edward VII was the only king to reign as a member of this house.

Edward VII (1901–10)

After whom the Edwardian period was named, Edward VII was much loved, very sociable, and a bit of a bon vivant. Edward's growing girth is said to have compelled him to leave the bottom button of his waist-coats open, a habit emulated by his peers and hangers-on and the source of the modern convention that a gentleman never fastens the lowest button on a single-breasted waistcoat.

 Edward the Seventh (1975, ITV; broadcast in the US as *Edward the King*)

THE WINDSORS

During World War I, nationalist hysteria was whipped up against all things German, and a family name like Saxe-Coburg-Gotha struck a lot of people as pretty darn German. So George V changed it to the quintessentially English "Windsor." (The grandfather of Queen Elizabeth II's husband, Prince Philip, anglicized his own surname from Battenberg to Mountbatten around the same time.) The Windsor surname now passes down to female heirs and their children, so, for example, Prince Charles takes his mother's, Queen Elizabeth's, surname and the dynasty goes on.

George V (1910–36)

On his deathbed, the king's doctor assured him that he would soon recover enough to go to his favored seaside resort, Bognor Regis. George's dying words supposedly were "Bugger Bognor" (though *The Times* reported them as "How is the Empire?" and his doctor reported the king exited with "God damn you" on being given a shot of morphine).

Edward VIII (January–December 1936)

His father prophetically said, "After I am dead, the boy will ruin himself in twelve months." Edward VIII gave up the crown to marry the American divorcée Wallis Simpson, which was no bad thing for the country as, though he was very handsome, he was quite conceited and had a soft spot for the Nazis.

 Edward and Mrs. Simpson (1978, ITV)

George VI (1936–52; last emperor of India, 1936–47)

Queen Elizabeth II's father and Edward VIII's brother. Shy and stuttering early in his reign, he and his consort Queen Elizabeth proved their mettle during the war, touring the bombed-out sections of London and making themselves visible.

 Bertie and Elizabeth (2002, ITV1)

Elizabeth II (1952–)

QEII rode the monarchy into the post-imperial age and made the Commonwealth matter. With her own children she was a little less fortunate, watching as they stumbled through their divorces and philandering under the gaze of the modern media. It might not always have looked good, but she did a remarkable job steering "The Firm" through unsteady times.

 *The Queen* (2006)

HOW TO IMPRESS OR INGRATIATE YOURSELF WITH BRITISH PEOPLE

- The subtle suggestion of money should do wonders. Forget the flashy Rolex, think more of the offhand reference to a third home in Portugal or showing up in a well-tailored suit with a custom-made shirt. Remember, subtle.

- Tell them how we couldn't have won "The War" (WWII) without them. The British take great umbrage at the suggestion that the American participation was somehow necessary for victory.

- Tell them how you find the restaurants in London to be superior to those of Paris. In fact, just about any opinion of British superiority to things foreign is taken warmly, however far-fetched or implausible it might be—that Blackpool beaches clearly outshine those of Barbados, for example.

- Mention how abysmal the British public transport system is. This is the one exception to the rule above.

- Invitations to visit will be well received. Caution: If you ask them, they will come.

- Most of all—don't try too hard.

HOW TO OFFEND A BRITISH PERSON

- Overt talk of money. Nobody needs to know how much you paid for your home, car, suit, or anything else. Houses are to be lived in, art is to be appreciated, and salaries are not to be discussed.

- Ask what they do for a living. It's not the worst question, but Americans insist on leading with it. It's not appropriate for a first conversation. Instead, start with an observation about the weather.

- Compliment the French. Ultimately, Brits are jealous that an entire country full of nobs got so much good stuff (food, wine, art, women, sun, and so on). They exhibit this jealousy by constantly making fun of the French and exact their revenge by taking extended holidays there.

- Ask if they know the royals or if anyone in their family has a title. Almost nobody you are going to meet does.

- Talk about how the Allies in World War II never would have won the war without help from America. "If it weren't for the US, you guys would be speaking German."

- Ask "Are you Australian?"

- Ask if it's terribly difficult living in the shadow of Europe. For that matter, if it's depressing living in a withered empire.

- Ask why they drive on the wrong side of the road. This question makes them defensive because the average British person has no idea why this is the case (see page 214).

- Mimic their accent and pepper your speech with words like "bloody," "fag," and "mate." (Let them get drunk and talk like J. R. Ewing or George W. Bush instead.)

- Ask "When did the UK last win the World Cup ... or anything?"

- Ask a Scottish person if Scotland is a suburb of London.

THE CHURCH OF ENGLAND

Some churches are born out of noble intentions and a desire to be closer to God. The Church of England was born out of Henry the VIII's desire to ditch his wife, Catherine of Aragon, and marry his mistress, Anne Boleyn.

England had stood by the Roman Catholic Church as it tried to suppress the new Protestant movement in Europe. That is, until a stubborn Pope Clement VII refused to annul Henry's marriage to Catherine of Aragon, who had failed to bear Henry a son. This refusal thwarted Henry's plans to marry the beguiling Anne Boleyn. Taking matters into his own hands, Henry pushed the British parliament to pass laws that, in 1534, created a new Church of England with the monarch of England at its head. As the leader of the church, Henry could now be the arbitrator of his own divorce and, of course, confiscate the vast wealth and holdings of the Catholic Church in England. It should be noted that under this arrangement, and to this day, there is no division between church and state in England.

For good measure, Henry also held on to the title Fidei Defensor (Latin for "Defender of the Faith") that a previous pope had bestowed on him for his pro-Catholic pre-divorce writings. Ironically for the leaders of a Protestant church, the kings and queens of England have continued to include this papal honorific in their full titles and on their coinage. Even today, if you look at any British coin you'll see the initials "FD."

Another legacy of this break and the bitterness it fomented over the following couple of hundred years was a whole raft of stridently anti-Catholic laws. Most, but not all, of these were repealed in the nineteenth century. Catholic bishops today regularly call for revocation of the 1701 Act of Settlement, which prohibits the monarch or heir to the throne from either becoming or marrying a Catholic. Despite this legislative anachronism, Catholics in mainland Britain, nicknamed "Left-footers" for obscure reasons, suffer no real social stigma or discrimination.

After the monarch, the Archbishop of Canterbury is the next most important figure, followed by the Archbishop of York and then the bishops who oversee the dioceses. In 1994, women were first ordained as priests in the Church of England, but that didn't help boost already low turnout at churches.

As the oldest Anglican church, and with the Archbishop of Canterbury as its executive leader, the Church of England is first among equals in the Anglican Communion, the worldwide body of independent churches with historical ties to the "C of E." In the US, Anglicanism is represented by the Episcopal Church, in Ireland by the Church of Ireland.

Like Christian congregations everywhere, the Church of England has divided between those who would like to evangelize and bring the faith to the masses and those who yearn for some real or imagined pageantry of the past. The evangelicals, who trace their tradition to Martin Luther and the complete Protestant breach from Rome, are labeled "happy-clappy" by their opponents in reference to their introduction of tambourines, hand-clapping, guitars, and such into the rites of worship. On the other side, the worship of so-called Anglo-Catholics, who regard themselves as members of a reformed Catholic church, is sometimes derided as "smells and bells" because of its fondness for incense and ritual. There are conservative and liberal wings on each side, though today the conservative evangelical tradition is pre-eminent.

The Church of Scotland is a separate entity from the Church of England. In 1560, the Scottish reformers abolished the authority of the pope in Scotland. In 1689, a constitutional act established Presbyterianism in Scotland under William and Mary.

HIGHLIGHTS OF THE SOCIAL SEASON

The Royal Horticultural Society's **Chelsea Flower Show** kicks off the summer season in London each May on the grounds of the Royal Hospital. The Chelsea Flower Show was first held in 1862, though the original venue was in Kensington, and it was called the Great Spring Show.

The **Royal Ascot** horse-racing event runs for a few days each June at the Ascot Racecourse just under an hour's drive west of London. The event started in 1768, and the monarch's own horses are likely to compete in it each year. While horse racing is, in theory, the focus of the event, fashion and who's who play a prominent role as well. Dress code depends on where you're sitting. The royal enclosure requires men to wear morning suits (see page 55) and women to wear hats and appropriately formal dresses (strapless dresses or exposed midriffs are not suitable). Those sitting outside the royal enclosure during Royal Ascot should dress smartly, though they don't need to don morning suits and formal attire. Ladies' Day at the royal enclosure is all about high fashion: hats, high heels, and, yes, some horses.

Wimbledon, which started in 1877 as a garden party tennis tournament, is now where the world's top-ranked tennis players convene each year to compete on grass courts. It runs from the end of June into early July in the London suburb of Wimbledon, which is accessible by London Underground or train from Waterloo station. The signature drink of Wimbledon is a Pimm's No. 1 Cup (see page 160).

The **Henley Royal Regatta** rowing races are held on the River Thames at Henley-on-Thames (west of London, between London and Oxford) each July. This annual rowing race started in 1839 and now runs for five days with qualifying races held beforehand. The reigning monarch is the patron of the event, hence the name Henley Royal Regatta.

The **Glyndebourne Festival Opera** is held in East Sussex every May through August. It was founded by John Christie and his wife, Audrey Mildmay, at the Christie family estate at Glyndebourne. The first opera was held in 1934. Going to see an opera at Glyndebourne is a formal affair: Men wear black tie and guests hold elaborate formal picnics on the grounds by the performance.

GOING TO A WEDDING IN THE UK

While it's probably not a good idea to generalize about all weddings in the UK, since like anywhere there are countless ways of doing it, we'll just point out some typical things about traditional UK weddings.

- The rehearsal dinner is an American convention. In the UK there might be a family dinner the night before a wedding, but not an event on the scale of the rehearsal dinners seen in the US.

- Toasts are made at the wedding (since there's no rehearsal dinner), and traditionally are made only by the father, or another representative, of the bride; the bridegroom; the best man; and now sometimes the bride as well.

- Traditionally women wore hats to weddings, and many women still do. These days, though, it's not mandatory. Since traveling with a hat is a total nuisance, don't bother unless you feel inspired.

- At a smart wedding, men wear morning suits—a cutaway tail coat with gray striped trousers and a waistcoat. If the wedding is the sort where these will be worn, you can either rent one— Moss Bros. is the classic place and has stores throughout the UK—or you could just wear a dark suit.

- The format of a traditional UK wedding is, generally speaking, a bit more relaxed than what is typical in the US, where weddings tend to be more extravagant.

- In Scotland, there may be bagpipes and men in kilts. Before donning a tartan, consider the following guidelines to avoid embarrassing yourself. For a wedding or public engagement, don't put on the kilt unless one or more of the following applies:

  > You were born in Scotland.
  > Both your parents are from Scotland.
  > You're a member of the royal family.

- Few Englishmen would dare wear a kilt in Scotland, and for good reason: They're likely to get beaten up. If you're purely a tourist, not attending a particular function, and don't care what the locals think, then go for it.

- Also, if you're in Scotland for a wedding, you should be prepared to dance reels. These are fun, complicated dances that will become easier after a few drinks, though more difficult after too many drinks.

SOCIETY FAQS

What's a "chav"?

A chav is a lower-class person, male or female, who has a penchant for expensive but not very tasteful clothes and jewelry. The term, considered derogatory, describes someone who tends to wear track suits, gold chains, big hoop earrings (for women), and Burberry tartan (which has become associated in the UK with chavs). Think of expensive cars, big prominent logos, drunken brawls, and antisocial behavior orders (ASBOs, see page 206). The tabloids have called Victoria and David Beckham, the model Jordan, former girl-group Atomic Kitten member Kerry Katona, and footballer Wayne Rooney and his wife, Coleen McLoughlin, chavs. The character Vicky Pollard on the hit show *Little Britain* is a chav. The word "chav" is said to be an acronym for "Council Housed and Violent," a council house being public housing in the UK, though there's no real evidence to support this.

What's a "toff"?

"Toff" describes someone who is upper-class, posh, and attended public (that is, private) school. It's insulting to call someone a toff. In politics, Conservative Party candidates in elections will sometimes get called toffs by their Labour opponents.

Who are "yobs" and "hoodies"?

Yobs are rowdy youth, generally boys, with a disregard for law and order. When you talk about "lager louts" and "football hooligans," these are part of the "yob culture" that has been held largely responsible for drunken violence in the UK.

A hoodie is a sweatshirt with a hood. The definition has expanded to include people who wear hoodies to conceal themselves from CCTV (closed caption TV, see page 209) or to intimidate. Some stores ban people wearing hoodies from entering.

What's a "mockney"?

A mockney is an upper-class person assuming a Cockney (see page 168) manner to gain street cred. Movie director Guy Ritchie, the singer Lily Allen, and the chef Jamie Oliver have all been called mockneys.

IMMIGRATION IN THE UK

Like many countries, the UK has experienced periodic waves of immigrants from different locations. In the 1950s, '60s, and '70s, for example, hundreds of thousands of people moved to the UK from the West Indies. Recently, there has been a tremendous influx of people from Eastern Europe, in particular Poland, Latvia, and Lithuania. In 2004, eight Eastern European countries joined the EU, which led to hundreds of thousands of Eastern Europeans moving to the UK for work. Some of these immigrants have already left the UK, and the rate of immigration from Eastern Europe is reported to be slowing down. Still, you might notice that your favorite brand of Polish beer has gotten a lot easier to find in recent years.

FACT OR FICTION?

British people love to hear about your British ancestry.
Fiction. Nobody cares that you're one-eighth Scottish, you're still American.

Almost all Englishmen have a bowler hat that they save for special occasions.
Fiction. Unless someone is dressing up in costume to look like an Englishman, bowler hats are rarely worn.

The title of baronet was created to raise cash.
Fact. While it is the newest of the titles currently on offer, the institution of the baronetcy owes its existence to one of the most ancient predicaments of kings, namely a desperate shortage of money. Strapped for cash, James I (or James VI and I, as they call him in Scotland) created this whole new rank between barons and knights in 1611 and promptly put the titles up for sale at an advertised price of £1,095. The scheme proved so popular that by 1625, they were going for

£3,000 (with sixteen thousand acres in Nova Scotia tossed in as a freebie).

Every swan in Britain is the personal property of the queen.
Fiction. Of course she doesn't own all the swans in the country. That would be ridiculous in this day and age! The crown gave up that long-held right in 1482 and now claims only all the mute swans that aren't marked as belonging to either the Worshipful Company of Vintners or the Worshipful Company of Dyers. Every summer the "swan uppers" put on their ceremonial costumes for the annual "swan upping" on specific stretches of the Thames where the offspring of the queen's and each company's swans are counted and marked accordingly. (The Dyers put a ring on one leg, while the Vintners put rings on both legs. Those swans with no rings are the queen's.) This tradition started because swans were delicacies for royal banquets; swan upping today is done more for conservation and education purposes.

No one in their right mind would give up a title.
Fiction. In 1963, legislation was enacted permitting a hereditary peer to disclaim his title without prejudicing his heir's rights to resuming the title. Peers populated the House of Lords but were not allowed in the House of Commons. The bill was passed solely for the benefit of left-wing firebrand Tony Benn, who found himself no longer able to sit in the House of Commons on inheriting his father's title of Viscount Stansgate. Funnily enough, that same year the Conservatives found a use for the new law, when retiring Tory prime minister Harold Macmillan's selected successor, the fifteenth Earl of Home (pronounced "Hume"), set aside his title to become Sir Alec Douglas-Home, enter the House of Commons, and lead the Conservatives to defeat in October 1964.

CHAPTER 3

CULTURE

WHAT YOUR NEWSPAPER SAYS ABOUT YOU

Those who believe that the cardinal virtue of a newspaper is objectivity will receive a rude awakening on landing in the UK. The British press makes little pretense toward evenhandedness. Be warned that the paper tucked under your arm flaunts your politics and social aspirations. On the Tube, in the pub, or on a park bench, as you join the legions of readers unfurling broadsheets like peacocks flourishing their plumage, consider what message you're sending out to the world as well as the angle on the news you're taking in.

The following is a brief synopsis of the major newspapers' politics and perceptions.

HIGHBROW NEWSPAPERS: BROADSHEETS

The Times

Referred to in the Victorian era as "The Thunderer" and the paper of record for much of its two-hundred-plus-year history, *The Times* has withered in the last couple of decades to become just another center-right, tabloid-sized fruit on Rupert Murdoch's tree. Think of *The New York Times* deteriorating into a tabloid version of *USA Today*.

The Daily Telegraph

The Daily Telegraph, or "The Torygraph" as it is known in reference to its right-wing politics, is the voice of the Establishment. Editorially it traditionally leans toward the "Little Britain" mind-set of the Conservative old guard. *The Daily Telegraph* takes itself as seriously as *The New York Times,* though its politics are more akin to *The Wall Street Journal.*

The Guardian

Formerly stodgy and doctrinaire in its left-wing stance, *The Guardian* has reengineered itself in the last decade to become the international liberal paper of record. It used to be so famously typo-ridden that the satirical magazine *Private Eye* nicknamed it "The Grauniad." Consider it similar to *The Washington Post,* but with a more liberal point of view. On Sunday *The Guardian* publishes as *The Observer.*

Financial Times

Printed on its signature broadsheet pink paper, the *Financial Times* is one of the world's most widely read daily financial newspapers. Started in 1888, it consumed or fended off competitors to become the leading business newspaper in Britain. It's comparable to *The Wall Street Journal,* though not nearly as conservative.

The Independent

The Independent is a left-wing broadsheet that was founded in 1986 by a gang of dissatisfied journalists from *The Daily Telegraph.* "The Indie," as it is nicknamed—the Sunday *Independent* being "The Sindie"—is dynamic, innovative, and iconoclastic. Middle East correspondent Robert Fisk is its star draw.

LOWBROW NEWSPAPERS: TABLOIDS

These are collectively known as "red tops" due to the predominant use of red ink in their mastheads.

The Sun .

The Sun has the highest circulation of any daily in Britain—and is one of the crown jewels in Rupert Murdoch's global newspaper holdings. Page 3 of *The Sun* famously features a different topless girl every day. In contrast to the old joke about the man who protests that he reads *Playboy* only for the articles, Page 3 is usually the most edifying thing in *The Sun*. Envision an even lower-brow version of the *New York Post*.

News of the World

The Sun's Sunday edition is the *News of the World,* a moniker it quite singularly fails to live up to. The front page is generally devoted to exposés on the infidelities, indiscretions, incarcerations, and intoxications of reality television "stars" and professional athletes. Its obsession with sex has earned the paper the nickname "the News of the Screws."

Daily Mirror

The *Daily Mirror* is the left-wing rival of *The Sun*. Famous for such headlines as "How can 59,054,087 people be so DUMB?" following George W. Bush's reelection in 2004, the *Daily Mirror* takes pride in being the voice of the working man. It's similar to a national version of the New York *Daily News* though is more celebrity studded. The Sunday edition is called the *Sunday Mirror.* The Scottish newspaper the *Daily Record,* which comes out on Sunday as the *Sunday Mail,* is published by the same company, Trinity Mirror PLC.

Daily Mail

The *Daily Mail* is the rant of the knee-jerk right-winger. In the Harry Potter books, Harry's small-minded uncle, Vernon Dursley, reads the *Daily Mail*. It actually covers world events and national political debate, so is a bit more highbrow than *The Sun*. If Rush Limbaugh and Dr. Laura were looking for a British audience, they'd probably find one here. The Sunday edition is *The Mail on Sunday*.

Daily Express

The *Daily Express* is a second-rate version of the *Daily Mail*. This assessment is borne out by the *Daily Mail*'s nearly three-to-one circulation advantage. The *Daily Express* has a pro-"values" stance, but finds itself compromised by the fact that its proprietor, Richard Desmond, made his fortune through such publications as *Big Ones, Posh Housewives,* and *Asian Babes*. The Sunday edition is the *Sunday Express*.

Daily Star

The *Daily Star* is a right-of-center paper mostly featuring scantily clad women, celebrity updates, and sports news. Started in the late 1970s, it has the third-highest circulation of national dailies after *The Sun* and the *Daily Mirror*. It's owned by Richard Desmond's Express Newspapers.

Evening Standard

Usually referred to as the *Standard,* this tabloid-format paper is distributed in and around London and southeast areas of England. It is one of the only evening papers in London, with four editions coming out during the day Monday through Friday. The paper sways a bit right of center politically. The *Standard*'s art critic Brian Sewell is famous for his denunciations of contemporary art.

GREAT BRITISH TABLOID HEADLINES

Copywriters at the British tabloids don't mince their words, and while they frequently forgo taste they do keep a sense of humor. Below are a few of the more famous tabloid headlines of recent times.

- The *Daily Mirror* on George Bush's 2004 reelection: "How can 59,054,087 people be so DUMB?"
- *The Sun* on EU Commission chairman Jacques Delors's 1990 calls for tighter European economic integration: "UP YOURS DELORS."
- *The Sun* on Elton John and David Furnish's 2008 wedding: "ELTON TAKES DAVID UP THE AISLE."
- *The Sun* after the British sank the Argentinean cruiser *General Belgrano* (killing more than 320) during the Falklands War: "GOTCHA."
- When France banned the sale of English lamb, *The Sun* responded: "HOP OFF YOU FROGS."
- The right-wing *Daily Express* on the new Labour prime minister Gordon Brown: "GORD HELP US NOW!"

MAGAZINES (AND THE CELEBRITY OBSESSION)

England has a centuries-long tradition of scurrilous and gossipy journalism. Some of the magazines keeping this tradition alive today are:

Hello!, cousin to the Spanish *Hola!,* is a feast of celebrity worship that revels in reality television "stars," footballers' wives, members of the royal family, and the usual A-list suspects for any paparazzi-fed publication. Since its coverage is invariably positive, it's a safe bet for celebs to cooperate for stories. *OK!* magazine is a similar read.

Heat, published by Bauer Media, is the full-on celebrity circus weekly magazine that, unlike *Hello!,* doesn't always have positive coverage of its subjects. *Heat* launched in 1999, and its circulation crept up to over half a million in its first decade. Credited with making celebrity culture in the UK even more popular than it was before, Heat radio and heat world.com have hit the air (and Internet) waves.

Tatler is a posh, smart, and glossy monthly magazine that focuses on society and fashion. It's now published by Condé Nast, and models itself after the original *Tatler,* which was started in the early 1700s as a magazine to amuse and inform the upper-classes. Tina Brown, of *Vanity Fair, The New Yorker,* and *Talk* magazine fame, edited *Tatler* from 1979 to 1983. Geordie Greig, who began as editor in 1999, oversees the two annual parties, the *Tatler* Summer Party and *Tatler*'s Little Black Book Party. Circulation is about ninety thousand, and contributing editors include such luminaries as Tom Wolfe, Toby Young, and Jerry Hall.

POLITICAL MAGAZINES OF NOTE

Private Eye is a biweekly satirical, humorous current affairs magazine edited by Ian Hislop. Filled with social and political observation as well as investigative journalism, the UK's top-selling news and current affairs magazine is famous for its convoluted references and inside jokes. Instead of drunk, they'll describe someone as "tired and emotional"; an illicit sexual escapade will be called "Ugandan discussions." These are typically based on somewhat ridiculous and embarrassing things people have said or done in the past. *Private Eye* is also known for being frequently sued for libel.

The Spectator is a conservative weekly magazine founded in 1828 that covers politics, the economy, and literary happenings. It's known for its essays and critical reviews. By comparison, it's something like the *National Review.* Globe-trotting socialite Taki writes the "High Life" column. Toby Young, author of the book *How to Lose Friends and Alienate*

People: A Memoir, is another contributor. The late Jeffrey Bernard wrote the legendary "Low Life" column documenting his many colorful escapades. The magazine's former editors include Boris Johnson, mayor of London.

New Statesman is a left-wing political weekly—*The Spectator* is its right-wing rival. Founded in 1913 by Sidney and Beatrice Webb, the magazine embraced their socialist leanings and intellectual bent. It has attracted a distinguished selection of writers over the years, such as Christopher Hitchens and Martin Amis.

BRITISH LIBEL LAWS

Very broadly speaking, libel is false information that is published and that damages a person's or a business's reputation. That seems straightforward enough—though the difference between libel laws in the US and the UK is quite dramatic.

In the US, the burden of proof is on the plaintiff in a case. The one who feels defamed must, as a general matter, prove that what was published was both untrue and written with the requisite degree of fault. When a public figure sues a media defendant such as a magazine or newspaper, for example, the plaintiff is required to prove "actual malice," a very high standard that results in many fewer high-profile plaintiffs' victories in the US than in Britain.

In the UK, however, it's the defendant who has to prove that libel was not committed, which is difficult to do. For example, if a writer says that a man hired a prostitute, then that writer has to prove in court that he did. It's also generally not necessary to prove malicious intent in Britain. Because the British libel laws favor the plaintiff to such a degree, foreigners often bring cases to British courts, because they know the odds are stacked in their favor. Furthermore, the loser of a case has to pay the winner's legal fees in addition to any other awards.

If a book is published in the US, but even a handful of copies are sold in the UK, the author can be sued for libel in UK courts. Thus, even US publishers have to watch out for potential libel suits in the UK. The following are a few examples of well-known British libel cases.

Oscar Wilde Libel Case

If only he'd just let it be . . . Oscar Wilde, a successful Irish-born novelist, poet, and playwright of the second half of the nineteenth century, was known for his long hair, eccentric manner of dressing, and bon mots. Wilde's close friendship (read: affair) with Lord Alfred Douglas caused Lord Alfred Douglas's father, the Marquess of Queensbury, a lot of concern. When the Marquess of Queensbury left a card for Wilde at his club, addressed to "Oscar Wilde . . . somdomite" [sic], Wilde made the mistake of suing him for libel.

When the evidence against Wilde was trotted out, he was arrested and found guilty of "gross indecency." Had Wilde just left it alone and not filed the libel suit, he wouldn't have gone to prison.

Jeffrey Archer Libel Case

Another libel suit that opened a Pandora's box was the well-known case of Jeffrey Archer. He came from humble beginnings, and in 1969, at age twenty-nine, he was elected to a seat in the House of Commons. Facing likely bankruptcy, he resigned from Parliament in 1974. However, he soon began writing bestselling novels, which made him a fortune. Shortly after being appointed as the Conservative Party deputy chairman, Archer sued the *Daily Star* in 1987 for libel after they reported he had hired a prostitute. Archer won the libel case and was awarded £500,000. The judge had taken a shine to Lord Archer's wife, and in his summing up to the jury he famously said that he couldn't imagine why a man with such a "fragrant" wife would hire a prostitute.

Prime Minister John Major made Archer a peer in 1992 for his fund-raising efforts on behalf of displaced Kurds. In 1999, the *News of the World* reported that Lord Archer had asked a friend to fake an alibi for him in the libel case against the *Daily Star*. Lord Archer was subsequently found guilty of having faked an alibi as well as faking diary entries to prove his innocence. Lord Archer spent about two years in prison and has continued to write novels.

Restaurant Review Libel

A libel case that caused alarm for restaurant critics in the UK and beyond was a suit brought against *The Irish News* in Belfast by the owner of an Italian restaurant who said a review of his establishment was "defamatory, damaging and hurtful." Journalist Caroline Workman in 2000 described the restaurant's chicken marsala as "so sweet as to be inedible" and said the staff was unhelpful and the cola flat. A Belfast jury decided in favor of the restaurant owner and awarded him £25,000. Claiming that this was an infringement of the freedom of the press, *The Irish News* appealed and the Northern Ireland court of appeals overturned the decision. Restaurant critics everywhere breathed a collective sigh of relief.

THE CELEBRITY CULTURE

It's a given that the US has a booming celebrity culture in which Paris, Britney, and the latest *American Idol* take center stage. It would be wrong, though, to assume that the US has cornered the market on it. The UK has a celebrity culture and then some—call it a celebrity obsession or a cult of celebrity. Footballers, their wives and girlfriends, reality TV "stars," and talent show contenders bask in the glow of warrantless fame for the sake of fame, with a big boost coming from celebrity magazines such as *Heat* and the many tabloid newspapers that cover their every move.

Katie Price, aka Jordan

She's just about everywhere in the UK celebrity circus. Starting out as a Page 3 girl (see page 61) she took on the modeling name "Jordan" and graced the pages of such illustrious publications as *Playboy*, *FHM*, and *Maxim*. Just in case there is any question: Her ample bosom isn't real.

From there she's built an empire centered on her, her life, and her lifestyle. She's the author of three bestselling autobiographies: *Being Jordan: My Autobiography; Jordan: A Whole New World;* and *Jordan: Pushed to the Limit.* Not bad for someone who's only recently turned thirty. Additionally, she's written, under her real name, Katie Price, a children's book, *Mermaids and Pirates,* and three novels: *Angel, Crystal,* and *Angel Uncovered.* She's got a line of linens, designs lingerie and swimwear, has a fitness DVD, appears on a number of reality TV programs, has a perfume, and is launching a singing career. On top of it all, she is married to Australian pop star Peter Andre and is mother to several kids.

Kerry Katona

The turbulent life of Kerry·Katona has included a difficult childhood (she lived with four different sets of foster parents), divorce from her first husband, a second marriage, depression, drug problems, a diagnosis of bipolar disorder, and bankruptcy—and the media have lapped it all up. Katona, born in 1980, found fame as a member of the girl group Atomic Kitten, though she left the group in 2001 to have her first child. Since then, she's gone on to host a number of television shows, win the reality show *I'm a Celebrity . . . Get Me Out of Here!,* and write her autobiography, *Too Much, Too Young: My Story of Love, Survival, and Celebrity,* three novels, and a column for *OK!* magazine. She was voted "Celebrity Mum of the Year" and later accused of doing cocaine while pregnant with her fourth child, a charge she vehemently denies. MTV UK's reality program *Crazy in Love* chronicled her daily life, and her recent breast reduction surgery was filmed for television—all this, apparently, being very interesting to a significant body of fans.

Posh and Becks

There's not much to say about Victoria and David Beckham that hasn't already been said. They seem to have fully permeated the US celebrity world as well as the UK's. Since Becks was the captain of the English national football team, though, there's an added dimension to their celebrity in the UK given the national passion for the sport. The UK now has oodles of mini-me versions of Posh and Becks running around—all the footballers and their WAGs (wives and girlfriends) trying to be like the Beckhams. Footballer Wayne Rooney and his wife Coleen Rooney (née McLoughlin) for example fill tabloid pages with news of their shopping trips, their multimillion-dollar wedding, and so forth.

CELEBRITY ROUNDUP

The most American British celebs
Sting
Elton John
Princess Diana
Richard Branson
Simon Cowell

Americans the Brits have taken to heart
Chrissie Hynde
Linda McCartney
Terry Gilliam
John Paul Getty
Bill Bryson
John Singer Sargent
Kevin Spacey
John McEnroe

Brits whom the Brits are happy to see the back of
and Americans seem to embrace
Sarah, Duchess of York (Fergie)
Heather Mills
Paul Burrell

BOOK PUBLISHING

The UK has a long and illustrious history of book publishing. Many of the classics read today in the US originally came from the UK, from Charles Dickens's oeuvre to the Harry Potter series.

A FEW BESTSELLING UK AUTHORS YOU MAY NOT HAVE HEARD OF

Enid Blyton (1897–1968)

The word "prolific" does not do justice in describing England's beloved children's writer Enid Blyton: She wrote more than six hundred children's books, poems, and plays. Some of her best-known works are the Famous Five, Secret Seven, and Mystery series. She also wrote the Little Noddy series as well as the Malory Towers and St. Clare's series. Her books have sold more than three hundred million copies, and her stories are a fixture in the libraries and imaginations of generations of Brits.

Barbara Cartland (1901–2000)

She's called "the queen of romance." To speak of the oeuvre of the late romance novelist Barbara Cartland as "written" might be taken to bestow on them a degree of literary achievement beyond their mark, so instead we'll simply say that over a long career Dame Barbara "generated" more than seven hundred romance titles. In her stories, the classes always knew their places, and heroes and heroines were always chaste before their wedding night—all of which resulted in her generating sales of almost seven hundred million books.

Catherine Cookson (1906–98)

The illegitimate child of an impoverished alcoholic mother, Catherine Cookson wrote more than ninety historical novels that have sold more than one hundred million copies worldwide. All her stories take place in industrial northeastern England in an area now dubbed "Cookson Country." Many of her books have been turned into television miniseries starring such well-known actors as Catherine Zeta-Jones. One of Britain's richest women, Catherine Cookson was knighted, and so became Dame Catherine. She is particularly well known for the Mallen Trilogy.

Jilly Cooper (b. 1937)

Her bestselling novels have been called "bonkbusters" and "Aga sagas," referring to the large, expensive ovens found in the cozy country kitchens of the well-to-do who populate her novels. Whatever you call Jilly Cooper's popular fiction, she's sold more than eleven million books in the UK alone and continues to entertain legions of readers with her steamy stories of seduction and love triangles. She was a columnist at *The Sunday Times,* then later wrote a column for *The Mail on Sunday.* Her first romance novels came out in the 1970s and were simply titled with posh women's names: *Emily, Bella, Imogen, Prudence,* and *Octavia.* Her other novels include *Riders, Rivals, Polo,* and *The Man Who Made Husbands Jealous,* all of which were bestsellers.

TOP LITERARY PRIZES

Founded in 1971, the **Costa Book Awards** (formerly the Whitbread Book Awards) are one of the major annual literary events in the UK. There are five categories: first novel, novel, biography, poetry, and children's book. The author in each winning category receives £5,000. Authors must have been a resident of the UK or Ireland for at least six months of each of the previous three years to be considered, and the book must be published first in the UK or Ireland. Costa Coffee is a brand based in the UK, and Whitbread PLC is a large hotel and restaurant group in the UK that also sponsored the Whitbread Round the World Sailing Race (now sponsored by Volvo).

Since 1985, the Costa/Whitbread Book Awards have named a Book of the Year, selected from the five winners of the various categories. This prize includes an additional £25,000.

Recent Winners of the Costa Book of the Year Award

1999 *Georgiana, Duchess of Devonshire* by Amanda Foreman (biography)

2000 *English Passengers* by Matthew Kneale (novel)

2001 *The Amber Spyglass* by Philip Pullman (children's book)

2002 *Samuel Pepys: The Unequalled Self* by Claire Tomalin (biography)

2003 *The Curious Incident of the Dog in the Night-Time* by Mark Haddon (novel)

2004 *Small Island* by Andrea Levy (novel)

2005 *Matisse: The Master* by Hilary Spurling (biography)

2006 *The Tenderness of Wolves* by Stef Penney (first novel)

2007 *Day* by A. L. Kennedy (novel)

The **Man Booker Prize** (usually just called the Booker Prize), is awarded annually to a novel written by a citizen of the Commonwealth or the Republic of Ireland. A UK investment firm, the Man Group, sponsors the prize; the previous sponsor was Booker McConnell, a multinational company. The contest is judged each year by a different group of leading critics, academics, and writers. A "long list" of twelve to thirteen titles is released, followed by a "short list" of the six finalists. Bookies around the UK take bets on which title will win. The winning author receives £50,000.

Recent Winners of the Man Booker Prize

2000 *The Blind Assassin* by Margaret Atwood

2001 *True History of the Kelly Gang* by Peter Carey

2002 *Life of Pi* by Yann Martel

2003 *Vernon Little God* by DBC Pierre

2004 *The Line of Beauty* by Alan Hollinghurst

2005 *The Sea* by John Banville

2006 *The Inheritance of Loss* by Kiran Desai

2007 *The Gathering* by Anne Enright

2008 *The White Tiger* by Aravind Adiga

The Orange Broadband Prize for Fiction is awarded annually to a female novelist writing in English. An all-female panel judges the international contest, and authors from countries around the world have won it. First awarded in 1996, after there were no women on the Booker short list in 1995, the prize is £30,000. Some critics—both male and female—call the Orange Prize sexist, saying women are already a powerful force in publishing and shouldn't have their own award; they ask how people would feel if there were a men-only contest. The writer Auberon Waugh, son of Evelyn Waugh, called it the "Lemon Prize." Nonetheless, it has become a major book prize. There is also the Orange Broadband Award for New Writers, which is also just for women and has a prize of £10,000.

Winners of the Orange Broadband Prize for Fiction

1996 *A Spell of Winter* by Helen Dunmore

1997 *Fugitive Pieces* by Anne Michaels

1998 *Larry's Party* by Carol Shields

1999 *A Crime in the Neighbourhood* by Suzanne Berne

2000 *When I Lived in Modern Times* by Linda Grant

2001 *The Idea of Perfection* by Kate Grenville

2002 *Bel Canto* by Ann Patchett

2003 *Property: A Novel* by Valerie Martin

2004 *Small Island* by Andrea Levy

2005 *We Need to Talk About Kevin* by Lionel Shriver

2006 *On Beauty* by Zadie Smith

2007 *Half of a Yellow Sun* by Chimamanda Ngozi Adichie

2008 *The Road Home* by Rose Tremain

BRITISH LITERARY HEAVY HITTERS

Some Dead British Literary Legends of the Nineteenth and Twentieth Centuries

Charles Dickens (1812–70) Famously prolific Victorian era novelist whose stories include *A Christmas Carol, A Tale of Two Cities, Great Expectations, David Copperfield, Little Dorrit,* and *Our Mutual Friend.*

Robert Louis Stevenson (1850–94). Scottish writer whose books include *Kidnapped, Treasure Island*, and *Dr. Jekyll and Mr. Hyde*.

Arthur Conan Doyle (1859–1930). The Scottish creator of Sherlock Holmes. His other books include *Sir Nigel* and *White Company*.

Beatrix Potter (1866–1943). Her many timeless children's stories include *The Tale of Peter Rabbit, The Tale of Benjamin Bunny*, and *The Tale of Squirrel Nutkin*.

P. G. Wodehouse (1881–1975). He's the creator of Jeeves and Bertie Wooster. Say no more.

Agatha Christie (1890–1976). Her gripping murder mysteries include *Murder on the Orient Express, Death on the Nile, Murder at the Vicarage, The Mysterious Affair at Styles,* and many others.

J. R. R. Tolkien (1892–1973). A fantasy writer famous for *The Hobbit* and *The Lord of the Rings*.

C. S. Lewis (1898–1963). A scholar and a Christian convert, he was author of the seven-part series the Chronicles of Narnia as well as *The Screwtape Letters, The Problem of Pain, Out of the Silent Planet, Perelandra, That Hideous Strength,* and many others.

Evelyn Waugh (1903–66). A brilliant satirist whose books include *Decline and Fall, Vile Bodies, Black Mischief, A Handful of Dust, Scoop,* and *Brideshead Revisited*.

Ian Fleming (1904–68). The creator of James Bond. His books include *Casino Royale, Dr. No, Goldfinger, From Russia with Love,* and, rather curiously, *Chitty Chitty Bang Bang*. Ian Fleming's brother was travel writer Peter Fleming.

Graham Greene (1904–91). Prolific novelist, journalist, and play-wright. He wrote *Stamboul Train, The Third Man, Brighton Rock, The Power and the Glory, The Heart of the Matter, The End of the Affair, The Quiet American, Our Man in Havana,* and more.

Roald Dahl (1916–90). A Welsh writer known for his dark stories for adults and children that include *Someone Like You, James and the Giant Peach,* and *Charlie and the Chocolate Factory.*

Kingsley Amis (1922–95). A famous alcoholic whose novels include *Lucky Jim, That Uncertain Feeling, The Green Man, Jake's Thing,* and *The Old Devils.*

Alive (as of This Writing) British Literary Heavy Hitters

V. S. Naipaul (b. 1932). Trinidadian born, Nobel Prize–winning author. His books include *A House for Mr. Biswas, In a Free State, Guerrillas, A Bend in the River, India: A Wounded Civilization,* and *A Way in the World.*

Philip Pullman (b. 1946). Author of the bestselling trilogy *His Dark Materials* and the novel *The Scarecrow and His Servant.*

Salman Rushdie (b. 1947). Anglo-Indian novelist whose books include *The Satanic Verses, Midnight's Children, The Moor's Last Sigh, The Ground Beneath Her Feet,* and *Shalimar the Clown.*

Ian McEwan (b. 1948). Dark humor and spare prose characterize his books, which include *The Cement Garden, The Comfort of Strangers, The Child in Time, The Innocent, Black Dogs, Amsterdam, Atonement, Saturday,* and *On Chesil Beach.*

Martin Amis (b. 1949). Son of Kingsley Amis. His books include *The Rachel Papers, Other People, Night Train, London Fields, Time's Arrow,* and *House of Meetings.*

Kazuo Ishiguro (b. 1954). Japanese-born author whose books include *A Pale View of Hills*, *An Artist of the Floating World*, *The Remains of the Day*, and *The Unconsoled*.

J. K. Rowling (b. 1965). Creator of Harry Potter and his world.

Zadie Smith (b. 1975). A young literary sensation, she has written the novels *White Teeth*, *On Beauty*, and *The Autograph Man*.

BRITISH NOBEL LAUREATES IN LITERATURE

1907 Rudyard Kipling (1865–1936)

1932 John Galsworthy (1867–1933)

1948 T. S. Eliot (1888–1965). He was born in the US but became a British citizen.

1950 Bertrand Russell (1872–1970)

1953 Sir Winston Churchill (1874–1965)

1981 Elias Canetti (1905–94). He was born in Bulgaria but immigrated to England prior to World War II.

1983 William Golding (1911–93)

2001 V. S. Naipaul (b. 1932). He was born in Trinidad but moved to England after attending the University of Oxford.

2005 Harold Pinter (b. 1930–2008)

2007 Doris Lessing (b. 1919). She was born in Persia (Iran) and lived in Zimbabwe, then called Rhodesia, until settling in England in her early thirties.

GAY LIFE

WHERE DO GAY PEOPLE GATHER?

London is often said to be the gay capital of Europe, with an active gay scene, a buzzing nightlife, and numerous memorials to Princess Diana.

Gay and lesbian London centers on Soho in the West End, though there are still gay establishments in Earl's Court, once the hub of London's gay nightlife, such as the famous Coleherne pub. A number of gay clubs and businesses have opened in recent years in Vauxhall, just south of the Thames. For lesbians, Stoke Newington in northeast London is an alternative to Soho.

Outside London, every British city has its own gay scene nowadays, though none matches that of Brighton, on the south coast sixty miles from London. This resort city has a long gay history and attracts gays and lesbians from all over the country, particularly to the "gay village" of Kemptown.

GAY FAQS

Is there same-sex marriage in the UK?
No, though the Civil Partnership Act went into effect throughout the UK in December 2005. Both partners must be at least sixteen years old and can't already be married or in a civil partnership. Like in the US or any country, a civil partnership provides a same-sex couple with more legal rights than two people just living together would have. There is no gay marriage at this point in the UK.

Who are some gay icons of the UK?
Kylie Minogue
Dusty Springfield
Ian McKellen
Oscar Wilde
Freddie Mercury
Madonna
Daniel Craig
Quentin Crisp
David Beckham

SPORTS

SPORTING DIFFERENCES

Globalization has raised awareness of American sports in the UK, though you might find the locals' opinions colored by native comparisons. To most British people, for example, baseball looks to be grown men playing a variant of the children's game rounders (from which baseball is thought to be descended). Likewise, views on the manliness of basketball might be prejudiced by its similarity to the schoolgirls' game netball. You can, of course, take consolation in the knowledge that Britain is a country where darts is a televised professional sport with an actual following.

FOOTBALL

Like the Brazilians, Italians, Turks, and others throughout the world, the British love football, deeply, passionately. And by "football," we mean soccer; the game played by the NFL is referred to as "American football." The game is deeply embedded in the national sense of identity. Almost every schoolboy dreams of growing up to play for one of the big teams, known as "clubs." The British do, after all, claim credit for inventing the game.

The intense tribalism of the British that Caesar wrote about more than two thousand years ago is still alive in the loyalty of the working-class fans to their local teams. Infamously, this devotion has all too often overflowed into violence and hooliganism, though the worst of those days have hopefully passed, having peaked in the late 1980s. Still, visitors attending a "match," as games are called, will likely be surprised to find the home and visiting teams' supporters segregated into different seating sections, depending on which team they bought their tickets through. Don't be overly alarmed, though: There has been a real push in the past decade to make a trip to the match more family friendly. You might say attending a league game has gone from an R-rated to a PG-rated outing.

During a match, the fans will burst into song. These "chants" are a colorful part of football and, to a lesser extent, rugby matches. With tunes derived from hymns and pop songs, chants can serve to boast of a team's prowess, such as the Chelsea fans' anthem "Carefree," chanted to the music of the hymn "Lord of the Dance"; to mock an opponent, as when the fans of anyone playing Liverpool burst into "Feed the Scousers," sung to the tune of "Do They Know Its Christmas?"; to chastise a referee, as when fans break into "Who's the Bastard in the Black?"; or simply to celebrate success, like West Bromwich Albion's shouts of "Boing, Boing" on scoring a goal, or the universal call of "Can we play you every week?" on an easy victory. Other songs have been appropriated in their entirety: Americans might think of the musical *Carousel* when they hear the Rodgers and Hammerstein standard "You'll Never Walk Alone," but in England it's known as the Liverpool FC anthem.

The Teams

In England, football is overseen by the Football Association, universally referred to as the FA. In Scotland, the game is overseen by the Scottish Football Association; in Northern Ireland, the Irish Football Association; and in Wales, the Football Association of Wales (or the utterly unpronounceable Cymdeithas Bêl-droed Cymru, in the Welsh language). Each of these organizations runs its own leagues (though the best Welsh teams will actually play in the English leagues) meaning that, by and large, the only time the different nations' clubs will face off against one another is in European competition, where teams from all across the continent compete.

Within each nation, teams are divided into a hierarchal series of leagues. There was a time when these divisions had simple, easy-to-understand names. For example, English teams were ranked into the First, Second, Third, and Fourth divisions. But now corporate sponsorship, squabbles over television rights, and the vicissitudes of professional athletics have done away with such a straightforward system. Today's English divisions are, in descending order: the Premier League; the Football League Championship, usually shortened to the Championship; Football League One; and Football League Two. Sports being sports and sponsorship being what it's all about, the actual full current names of the top two England leagues are the Barclay's Premier League and the Coca-Cola Football League Championship. Scotland is a little simpler, with a Scottish Premier League trailed by a First, Second, and Third Division.

FOOTBALL DIVISIONS

England	Scotland
Premier	Scottish Premier
Championship	First Division
Football League One	Second Division
Football League Two	Third Division

Through an ever-extending season—it starts in August with the FA Community Shield and ends in late May with the FA Cup—teams within a division battle it out on the pitch (the field). At the end of the season, the teams at the bottom of the league are relegated to a lower division and replaced by the top teams from the league below.

Over time, once-great teams, like Nottingham Forest, have slipped out of the top divisions, while former also-rans, such as Fulham, have ascended. Through the years, though, a handful of teams have consistently excelled. Any list of these would have to include Liverpool, Manchester United, and London's Arsenal and Chelsea clubs. In Scotland, Glasgow's two rival teams, Celtic and Rangers, have proven their staying power.

The Big Games

Just as the Super Bowl dominates American sports, the FA Cup Final is the single biggest fixture in the entire English (and, frankly, British) sports calendar. Competition for the FA Cup runs as a knockout tournament alongside regular season games with all the teams in the four English divisions, plus a few others, competing. Eventually, only two teams remain to face off in the Cup final, always played at London's Wembley Stadium.

Unlike the winners of the Super Bowl and the World Series, the winner of the FA Cup does not presume to declare themselves "World Champions." That title can only be worn by the current holder of football's World Cup. The World Cup is held every four years and is indisputably the largest global sporting event, though it might hardly seem that way to US viewers. Pre-tournament qualifying matches whittle the contenders down to thirty-two national teams, who then play against one another in football stadiums throughout the hosting country. The UK suffers under competing as four distinct international teams: England, Northern Ireland, Wales, and Scotland (though often as not, England is the only team that will qualify). When conversation turns to the World Cup, you will appear very sage if you merely nod your head in thought and quietly declare that this next World Cup might just be the one to match 1966.

The other venues, beyond their regular leagues and league championships, in which British clubs might play are the European UEFA Champions League and the UEFA Cup. UEFA (pronounced you-AY-fuh) is the Union of European Football Associations, though its nearly sixty-country-strong membership stretches into Asia. English teams often do very well in European competition: In 2008, the final for the most prestigious European trophy, the Champion Clubs' Cup, saw two English teams, Chelsea and Manchester United, face off in Moscow.

1966 WORLD CUP

England's 4–2 overtime victory over West Germany at Wembley Stadium—England was the host nation—is still a great source of national pride. English football fans today serenade the Germans with such crass ditties as "Two World Wars, One World Cup" whenever the two teams meet (ignoring the fact that Germany has actually won the World Cup three times to England's single victory). People who weren't even born at the time will still reminisce about manager Alf Ramsey's "wingless wonders," Bobby Charlton's masterful play in the semifinals, Geoff Hurst's hat trick in the final, and the national euphoria when the queen presented England captain Bobby Moore with the trophy. Of course, that they're still going on about it only underlines the fact that England's national team has never again made it to the final of a World Cup in the decades since, let alone won.

Football Hooliganism

It's been dubbed the "English disease." The mayhem and violence that have a nasty way of following English football teams across the Channel is one of the country's less welcome exports. The supporters' gangs are known as "firms," with names such as the Chelsea Headhunters, Millwall Bushwackers, and West Ham's Inter City Firm. Some of the firms have been known to clash with an extraordinary array of knives, chains, and medieval-looking implements. (In the mid-1990s the US State Department red-flagged Millwall's South London grounds, warning tourists to steer clear.) Some firms are said to have neo-Nazi links, and even at its most enlightened, football culture has more than its fair share of bigotry.

The 1995 England-Ireland game held in Dublin had to be called off due to rioting after a mere twenty-seven minutes of play. Fortunately, fan violence has declined considerably from the dark days of the late

1980s, when English clubs were banned from all European competition following the 1985 Heysel Stadium disaster in Brussels, where thirty-nine fans of the Italian team Juventus were crushed to death attempting to flee from rampaging Liverpool fans.

Reforms, including the abolition of both standing-room-only terraces and pitch-side fencing, were introduced following the 1989 Hillsborough disaster, in which police crowd-control failure rather than hooliganism was deemed to have caused the deaths of ninety-six Liverpool supporters. Coupled with tougher punishments, alcohol restrictions, and the creation of a police Football Intelligence Unit, the specter of violence has been virtually eliminated from within the football grounds, though it does still go on outside, albeit to a lesser extent than in the past.

WAGs

When defining a WAG—short for wives and girlfriends (of football players)—it's easiest to offer a two-word definition: Victoria Beckham.

The wife of footballer David Beckham, Victoria, aka Posh Spice, is queen of, and certainly the most famous of, her ilk. Some telltale identifiers of the WAG include large designer sunglasses, trendy handbag, well-coiffed hair, couture labels, a love of publicity and shopping, and, of course, a footballer on her arm. Often, WAGs are working-class girls who are suddenly rolling in money and shamelessly living the high life. It's worth noting, though, that many of them, Victoria Beckham included, have had their own successful careers. The British tabloids are filled with the adventures and misadventures of WAGs.

In 2002, the television show *Footballers Wive$* debuted in the UK. Needless to say, it's a gripping drama filled with sex, partying, football, and expensive but not necessarily tasteful cars, clothes, houses, and lifestyles.

British Football Legends
David Beckham, 2000s
George Best, 1960s
Bobby Charlton, 1960s
Dixie Dean, 1930s
Paul Gascoigne (aka "Gazza") 1990s
Kevin Keegan, 1970s
Gary Lineker, 1980s
Stanley Matthews, 1950s
Bobby Moore, 1960s
Peter Shilton, 1980s

Some Basic Football Terminology

Manager. The equivalent of a coach on an American team.

Match. Football teams play matches, not games.

Pitch. Football is played on a pitch, not a field.

CRICKET

Cricket strikes many Americans as the quintessentially English field sport: the players smartly attired in their whites, the genteel pace of the game, and, to the uninitiated, the baffling rules and terminology. And though the Europeans would be inclined to consider marauding gangs of drunken football fans more characteristically English, the English themselves would agree with the Americans that cricket is a reflection of their national character. And besides, what could be more English than a game that stops for tea? To say something is "not cricket" is to describe it as backhanded, dishonorable, and ungentlemanly.

As with other sports invented in England—rugby and lawn tennis, for example—foreigners have truly mastered the game and now routinely rout the English. Cricket's appeal, however, is not as universal as football's; its popularity is confined almost exclusively to former British colonies. The Indians, Pakistanis, South Africans, Zimbabweans, Australians, New Zealanders, Bangladeshis, and West Indians are all madly keen on the game (though, strangely enough, the Scottish, Welsh, and Irish are not). It's a summer sport, with the season running from April through September.

What on Earth Are They Doing?

Cricket has some similarities to baseball—in particular, each team tries to score the highest number of runs. The teams alternate batting and bowling (pitching), with each turn called an innings (which is always plural even if you're talking about one innings). Two batsmen are on the field (called a pitch) at once, each defending one wicket, which comprises three knee-high stakes, called stumps, with grooved tops on which rest two sticks, called bails. The bowler "bowls" (a straight-armed pitch) to the batsmen facing him with the goal of knocking down the wicket, which is one of a few ways a batsman can be taken out.

If the batsman hits the ball and thinks he can safely make it to the other wicket, he and the other batsman start running. A run is scored when both batsmen successfully reach the opposite wickets. When the batsman hits the ball out of the playing area, he's hit a "six," for which he earns six runs. If the ball touches the ground within the pitch but then bounces or rolls out, he gets four runs. The phrase "to hit a six" is used colloquially for success beyond the cricket field, the same way someone would talk about "hitting a home run."

The fielders—whose positions carry such colorful names as square leg, gully, third man, silly mid-off, and fine leg—try to catch a ball before it bounces or throw the ball to knock down one of the wickets while the batsmen are running, both of which result in an out. A batsman is also out for "LBW" (leg before wicket) if it's determined that the ball would have hit the wicket if the batsman's leg wasn't in the way. In the spirit of gentlemanliness, an umpire cannot unilaterally declare a batsman out but must wait for the fielding team to ask for his call. Therefore, any time a wicket falls (or there's some other event that could result in an out), expect to hear loud calls of "Howzat?" ("How's that?") from the fielding team.

The Teams

Perhaps because the sport is of a more pastoral nature than football, where teams tend to represent urban centers, cricket clubs are by and large organized at the county level. So a matchup will typically be something like Surrey versus Somerset. That said, it is really at the international level that cricket attracts a serious audience. As with other sports, the national team comprises the best English players from the club teams (though with cricket, Welsh players can join the England team). The Cricket World Cup is held each year, with international teams competing.

One thing sure to strike those unfamiliar with the game is the sheer length of a full-on test match. Though there are other formats in which cricket is played, test cricket is considered the highest level of competition, sprawling out over up to five days. Test cricket is played by ten international teams that the International Cricket Council has deemed worthy of full test status, one of which is, fortunately, England. Lesser national teams generally have to make do with shorter versions—first-class matches are capped at three or four days' playing time, and one-day matches take just one day—though all of the day.

Acknowledging that not everybody nowadays has five spare days, or even one whole day, to spend watching a cricket match, what with jobs, families, and the commitments of the modern world, cricketing has introduced a very popular and considerably shorter format, Twenty20. With this format, a match takes about three hours, roughly the same as a baseball game.

Should you be invited to a cricket match, we recommend asking your host what sort of match it is and consult the following chart before committing yourself firmly:

Popular Cricket Formats

Match Type	Clear the Calendar for . . .
Test match	Five days
First-class	Three or more days
One-day	One day, but all of it
Twenty20	About three hours

LORD'S CRICKET GROUND

The mother ship of English cricket is Lord's, the most famous cricket field in the world—it is known as "the home of cricket." Situated in London's St. John's Wood neighborhood, Lord's is home to the MCC, the Marylebone Cricket Club, but also hosts two test matches and two one-day internationals every year, as well as various other high-profile championships. One famous "feature" of the field, which might well be considered a defect elsewhere, is the sizable slope of the pitch: the northwest side is some eight feet higher than the southeast.

The MCC museum at Lord's is the world's oldest sporting museum and holds such hallowed trophies as the Ashes urn, the prize for the biennial test series—the teams play five full test matches!—between England and Australia.

English Cricket Legends

Ian Botham, 1980s
Geoff Boycott, 1970s
Denis Compton, 1940s
Andrew "Freddie" Flintoff, 2000s
Graham Gooch, 1990s
W. G. Grace, 1880s
Wally Hammond, 1930s
Jack Hobbs, 1910s
Len Hutton, 1930s
Fred Trueman, 1950s

Some Basic Cricket Terminology

Delivery. A pitch, as we know it in baseball.

Crease. The batsman's safe area in front of the wicket.

Innings. Oddly always plural, it's a team's turn at batting.

Over. Six deliveries from the bowler.

Six. Like a home run in baseball, a six is when the batsman hits the ball out of the field of play.

Wickets. Three knee-high stakes, called stumps, with grooved tops on which rest two sticks, called bails. There are two wickets on a cricket pitch (field).

Wisden. The *Wisden Cricketers' Almanack,* published annually since 1864, is the cricket fan's bible, with statistics, essays, and fixtures.

RUGBY

Way back in 1823, during a football match at the boys' public school Rugby, a student by the name of William Webb Ellis reportedly caught the ball in his hands—then actually allowed in football—and proceeded to run with it toward the opposing goal, in violation of the rules as they then stood. Like most foundation myths, there is little real evidence to support the story, and no explanation is offered as to why the referee didn't simply penalize Webb Ellis for breaching the rules of the game. Either way, both forms of rugby—rugby union and rugby league—hold Webb Ellis to be the founder of their sport.

Rugby Union

Rugby union is the form of rugby you are probably familiar with and is the predominant form of the international game. This is the great sport of the British middle-classes (football is for the working-class, and cricket just about cuts across class lines).

Teams

Like football, rugby, or "rugger" as it's sometimes called, is played domestically in ranked leagues with a season that runs from September through mid-May. In English rugby union, the top division is the Guinness Premiership, containing a dozen professional clubs. Beneath this are National Divisions One, Two, Three North, and Three South, followed by a smattering of regional leagues. The winner of the National Division One each year is promoted to the Guinness Premiership, whose bottom team is relegated to the lower league. The league system originated in 1987, its introduction foreshadowing the then amateur sport's transformation into a professional one, an event that finally took place in 1995. Today, all the Guinness Premiership teams are professional, while the lower division teams are a mix of professional and semiprofessional. For Scottish, Welsh, and Irish teams, the Magners League is the top-flight division. The top teams in the Magners League and Guinness Premiership proceed to the Europe-wide competitions, the Heineken Cup and the European Challenge Cup.

You might have noticed something of a pattern in the sponsorships above; Guinness and Heineken are beer companies and Magners an Irish cider maker. While rugby has none of the fan violence of football, the culture of the game is notoriously boozy. School, university, and recreational rugby club players—"Rugger buggers" in the parlance—have a tendency to take great pride in their beer consumption and subsequent beery behavior, much like college football players in American culture.

Like cricket, rugby is most popular as an international game. As with other sports, England, Wales, and Scotland all have national teams. Since the middle-class associations of rugby raise it above working-class Irish sectarianism, Ireland is represented by a single team (unlike most sports in Ireland, which have separate northern and southern teams). In fact, this amicability extends even further: The British and Irish Lions team, comprising the best players from England, Wales, Scotland, and Ireland, periodically goes on tour, playing other international teams.

Every four years, the international teams duke it out for the William Webb Ellis trophy in the Rugby World Cup, the premier international competition for rugby union. The Rugby World Cup has been played only since 1987, so England can be proud of its one win and two second-place showings. (Wales achieved third place in 1987 and Scotland fourth in 1991.) The biggest annual international competition for the British teams is the Six Nations Championship, with England, Ireland, Scotland, Wales, France, and Italy competing for the Championship Trophy. When one team beats all of its opponents during the competition, they are said to have achieved a "grand slam." Within the main competition, various side trophies are contested: England and Scotland play for the Calcutta Cup, Scotland and Ireland for the Centenary Quaich, and England and Ireland for the Millennium Trophy. There is also the Triple Crown, awarded in the event that one of the home nations—England, Wales, Scotland, or Ireland—defeats all three of the others during the Six Nations.

For English rugby, Twickenham Stadium, in the West London suburb of Twickenham, is its spiritual home. With seating for eighty-two
thousand, it is the largest stadium in the UK after Wembley. ("Twick-
ers" has also hosted rock concerts in recent years for bands such as the
Rolling Stones and U2.) In Scotland, the big rugby games are played at
Edinburgh's Murrayfield Stadium, and in Wales at Cardiff's Millennium
Stadium.

British Rugby Union Legends

Bill Beaumont, 1980s

Phil Bennett, 1970s

Will Carling, 1990s

Jonathan Davies, 1980s

Gareth Edwards, 1970s

Gavin Hastings, 1980s

Jonny Wilkinson, 2000s

J. P. R. Williams, 1970s

Rugby League

"Football is a gentleman's game played by ruffians; rugby is a ruffians'
game played by gentlemen; rugby league is a ruffians' game played by
ruffians," or so an old saying rather snobbishly states. In the north of
England, when people refer to rugby, they usually mean rugby league.
The roots of rugby league lie in rugby union. The Northern Rugby
Football Union split from the Rugby Football Union at the end of the
nineteenth century. Over time, the two branches developed different
rules, so that nowadays league and union are distinctly different games.
Rugby league was a professional sport from the get-go, instantly damn-
ing it to working-class status in the late Victorian mindset.

Despite this, league is actually a little less rough-and-tumble than
union, with more emphasis on tackling and less on mauls and scrums
to determine possession. In league, a team holds the ball for a "set of
six" tackles before turning it over, not dissimilar to downs in American
football. Scoring is similar in the two versions of the game, with each

side aiming to score "tries" and "conversions," though in league the number of points earned for each is slightly lower, and each team has only thirteen players to a union team's fifteen.

In addition to the north of England, rugby league is played in Australia, New Zealand, France, and Papua New Guinea, where it is officially recognized as the national sport. Internationally, Australia dominates the sport.

BETTING IN THE UK

The world of betting and bookies is much more legitimate and widespread in the UK than in the US. In the UK, you can pop into Ladbrokes or William Hill, two big bookies with branches throughout the country, and place a bet on who will win the Mercury Prize, the next election, or even the next round in a particular reality TV show. Horses, football, darts, snooker, cricket, tennis, rugby, and, of course, the greyhounds, are all fair game as well.

THE FOX-HUNTING BAN

Fox hunting is a tradition deeply rooted in the countryside of England. You'll often see images of red-coated huntsmen on horses, surrounded by a pack of hounds, on place mats and in prints depicting the quintessential English countryside (captions will read something like "Tally-ho!"). The thing is, though, that Britain is also home to an above-average concentration of animal lovers—the kind of people who go to great lengths to make sure an innocent fox isn't torn to bits by a pack of excited hounds.

And so there is the highly contested ban on fox hunting, which came into force in February 2005 in England and Wales. A similar bill was passed a bit earlier by the Scottish parliament. It is clearly a class thing—fox hunting is a sport of the upper-classes. The Hunting Act, as it's called, is not an outright ban on fox hunting; rather, it restricts the ways a fox can be hunted. For example, it's still legal to exercise hounds and use them to chase an artificial trail, or scent, which is called a "drag." Hounds can be used to flush out a fox but not kill it; the fox may be shot, or killed by a bird of prey, however.

Critics of the ban argue that it's an unenforceable law filled with loopholes. Who's to say the hounds weren't just exercising when they happened to get the scent of a real fox? It's rare that anyone is prosecuted for breaking the law, and, perhaps because the British have a natural rebellious streak, more people than ever hunt foxes since the ban went into effect; this is especially true on Boxing Day, December 26, one of the biggest days for hunting in the UK.

The Hunting Act was passed by the Labour majority in Parliament and is very much a Labour initiative. The Conservative Party has taken a stand against the ban. While the fox-hunting ban is mostly a city versus country issue, the fox itself makes no such distinctions. On a late-night walk through London, you're more than likely to spot a few foxes snooping around garbage bins and darting into parks.

SNOOKER

As some might say of pool players, a talent for snooker indicates a mis-spent youth. After all, snooker halls are dark, smoky places. Two notable things about professional snooker are that watching it on TV is exceptionally boring (it makes golf look exciting), and the uniforms are exceptionally interesting. Players wear waistcoats (the sleeveless and collarless vests worn over a shirt and under a dinner jacket) with sponsors' names emblazoned on the breast. It's almost like the players are wearing half a tuxedo—as if they just stepped away from some smart party and took off their jacket.

Snooker is a variation on billiards that developed in the late nineteenth century. The table is quite large, measuring twelve feet by six feet. There's one white cue ball, fifteen red balls, and six other balls in varying other colors, each worth a different number of points. The balls must be sunk in a particular order; when a red ball is pocketed it stays in the pocket, whereas the other colored balls are returned to the table as long as there still are red balls in play. "Snooker" is when the cue ball is in such a position that the player is unable to directly hit the ball that he's required to hit. The maximum number of points that can be scored on a break is 147—which is a major achievement.

The World Snooker Championship is held each year in Sheffield at the Crucible Theatre—the highlight of the snooker year. The sport is also popular in Asia.

British Snooker Legends
Joe Davis, 1920s, 1930s
Steve "Boring" Davis, 1970s, 1980s, 1990s
Stephen Hendry, 1980s, 1990s
Alex "Hurricane" Higgins, 1970s, 1980s
Ronnie O'Sullivan, 2000s

DARTS

Professional darts is indeed a televised sport in the UK. To the first-time viewer, what is most notable is the player's ability to hold a full pint of beer and a cigarette while throwing a dart. When televised, the screen is typically split, so you see the player on one side and the dart board on the other.

Each player throws three darts in a turn. A dartboard is divided into twenty sections, like slices of cake, valued at 1 through 20 points. The bull's-eye is worth 50 points, the outer bull's-eye ring worth 25, and, moving out from the center, there's a wide single-scoring ring, a thin triple-scoring ring, another wide single-scoring ring, and a double-scoring ring at the outside. The game starts at a number, often 301 or 501, and the points earned in a turn are subtracted—the first to get to 0 wins. A player has to hit 0 exactly to win. In a pub, or during an informal game, players might just add up the total points from each turn, starting at zero, until one of the players reaches a predetermined number.

TENNIS

Tennis is another one of those sports that the English are thought to have invented but which other nations now regularly beat them at.

British Tennis Legends
Sue Barker, 1970s
Tim Henman, 1990s, 2000s
Andy Murray, 2000s
Fred Perry, 1930s
Virginia Wade, 1970s

FACT OR FICTION?

If England is playing another country, such as France, in a football match, a Scottish person will probably be rooting for France to win.

Fact. Scottish sentiments toward England can be summed up by the tendency of Scots to root for teams playing against England. The Scots famously support "ABE" (anyone but England). A Welsh sports fan will also probably want England to lose the match. In the collective Scottish (and Welsh) psyche, centuries-old grudges and recriminations of occupation and defeat still linger just below the surface.

In a football match between Scotland and another country, such as France, an English person will probably be rooting for France to win.

Fiction. An English person will probably be rooting for Scotland to win. The English have rosier memories of their history with the Scottish, Welsh, and Irish than vice versa.

Manchester United, one of the world's biggest sports franchises, is known for the large number of fans it has in its hometown of Manchester.

Fiction. Manchester United is known for not having many fans in its hometown of Manchester. Mancs (people from Manchester) largely disdain the flashy Man U team, giving their allegiance to the city's other football team, Manchester City.

Paul Gascoigne, aka "Gazza," is one of England's most famous football players. Sadly, he suffers from mental health and addiction issues.

Fact. Gazza is one of England's most talented and beloved footballers, though since retiring from football he has regularly appeared in the tabloids for his battles with drinking and depression. He first played for the England national team in 1988 and for the last time in 1998.

The Chelsea football team is sometimes affectionately called "Chelski" because a number of the players are also on the UK Olympic skiing team.

Fiction. The team is sometimes called Chelski, not so affectionately, by fans of other teams, because it is owned by Roman Abramovich, a Russian.

When someone refers to a professional athlete as having been "capped," it means supporters of a rival team have shot him in the kneecap.

Fiction. That would be "kneecapping," a popular extrajudicial punishment meted out by the IRA (Irish Republican Army) in the heyday of Northern Irish violence. In sports, a player earns a "cap" when he plays for a select team, most often a national team. Though actual caps are no longer awarded, it is not uncommon to read that such-and-such a player has so many caps; for example, the football player Peter Shilton earned 125 caps between 1970 and 1990. In school sports, caps are given to distinguished players, much like a varsity letter.

POP MUSIC

There are too many legendary British musicians to count—from David Bowie to Tom Jones to the Beatles to the Rolling Stones to Pete Townshend to Sid Vicious. This relatively small northern island has had a huge impact on the music industry. Not every British pop star crosses over to North America, though. Below are a few music legends in the UK who haven't found the same success in the US.

Kylie Minogue

In the US, Kylie Minogue is a pretty famous Australian pop star who makes semi-regular appearances in the tabloids and on the music charts. She's big, but she's not huge. In the UK and Australia, however, it's a different story: She's an icon in the way that Madonna is an icon, though without the controversy. One thing both artists have in common is number one hits in the 1980s, 1990s, and 2000s.

Kylie's 1985–88 role on the popular Australian soap opera *Neighbours,* also big in the UK, put her on the map. She kicked off her music career in 1987 and quickly rose to pop stardom with her album *Kylie.* In the 1990s she collaborated with artists such as Nick Cave and the Pet Shop Boys. While interesting, this experiment with indie music wasn't a big hit with her fans, and she soon returned to pop. A diminutive five feet tall, Kylie is admired for her elaborate stage shows and her sexy butt. As proof of how loved she is, she's the most played female artist on UK radio in the past twenty years.

In 2005, Kylie was diagnosed with breast cancer. After taking time off to recover, she resumed her tour schedule at the end of 2006. Her sister, Dannii, has jumped on the bandwagon and has her own singing career, though it is nowhere near the magnitude of Kylie's, and she has been a judge on the talent show *The X-Factor.*

Cliff Richard

That's Sir Cliff to you! So awe-inspiringly awful you can only love him, Cliff Richard has wheedled his way into the nation's heart with fifty years of terrible records. Originally touted as a British Elvis, he was more like a British Pat Boone (and like Boone, Cliff became a born-again Christian). Who could forget such schlock as the singles "Living Doll" (1959), "Summer Holiday" (1963), "We Don't Talk Anymore"

(1979), and the truly dire "21st Century Christmas" (2006)? Certainly not his legions of fans: Sir Cliff has had number one singles in the 1950s, '60s, '70s, '80s and '90s. So far in the 2000s, he has hit the number two slot.

Robbie Williams

Like Justin Timberlake, Robbie Williams got his start in a boy band then parlayed that success into something much bigger. Robbie Williams started out in 1990 at age sixteen with Take That, but he really made a name for himself when he left in 1995 to launch his solo career. He soon became the bestselling solo artist in the UK. Sure, Robbie Williams is mildly famous in the US, but in the UK he's a sensation.

His first two solo albums were *Life Thru a Lens* in 1997 and *I've Been Expecting You* in 1998. Both went to number one on the UK charts. A compilation of these two albums, *The Ego Has Landed,* was released in the US to introduce Robbie to American listeners. With a penchant for partying (having done some time in rehab) and a tall, dark, handsome physique, he's won buckets of awards and continues to be one of the biggest pop stars in the UK.

Marc Bolan

The father of glam rock is Marc Bolan (1947–77) and, though some Americans may be familiar with Bolan and his band T. Rex, in the UK he was huge—the music press called T. Rex in the early 1970s "bigger than the Beatles." Known for his short stature, permed hair, platform shoes, eye shadow, and flamboyant glam outfits, he set the course that David Bowie, for one, rode to international success. Born Mark Feld in London, Bolan joined the cult garage band John's Children in 1967. That same year, he formed the band Tyrannosaurus Rex, which would later be shortened to T. Rex. His biggest hit in the US was "Bang a Gong (Get It On)" and in the UK he topped the charts with albums *Electric Warrior* (1971), *The Slider* (1972), and *Tanx* (1973) and hit with singles "Hot Love," "Jeepster," "Telegram Sam," "Children of the Revolution," and "Solid Gold Easy Action," among others. With Gloria Jones (an American soul singer who recorded the original "Tainted Love") he had a son named Rolan Bolan. Marc Bolan was killed in a car crash in West London in 1977 at age twenty-nine. There is a shrine to him at the site of the crash.

Paul Weller

He's called "the Modfather," because he's just so darn mod. Paul Weller, born in 1958, proudly hails from working-class roots, is known for his lefty politics, and holds a firm place as a major music legend in the UK. He started the band the Jam when he was just fourteen years old, playing guitar, singing, and writing songs, with his father as the band's manager. After a few years of playing small venues, they hit it big in 1977 with a record deal and a growing following. This was the first wave of punk rock in the UK, and other hot bands at the time were the Sex Pistols, the Clash, and the Buzzcocks—though the Jam was the most popular in Britain. Singles like "Going Underground" and "A Town Called Malice" went straight to number one on the charts. Weller broke up the Jam in 1982 at the height of their fame and soon after formed the Style Council—an ill-advised idea to bring more soul and jazz into his music. After some early hits, the Style Council went downhill rapidly, eventually lost their recording contract, and broke up. Part of the legend of Paul Weller is the comeback he then pulled off. As a solo artist, he hit it big again in the mid-1990s, becoming an iconic influence on Britpop bands like Oasis and Ocean Colour Scene.

ELEVEN SONGS THAT SUM UP THE
ESSENCE OF LIFE IN BRITAIN

- "The Village Green Preservation Society" by the Kinks
- "That's Entertainment" by the Jam
- "Parklife" by Blur
- "Dedicated Follower of Fashion" by the Kinks
- "Penny Lane" by the Beatles
- "God Save the Queen" by the Sex Pistols
- "Baggy Trousers" by Madness
- "London Calling" by the Clash
- "Nothing Ever Happens" by Del Amitri
- "Common People" by Pulp
- "Up the Junction" by Squeeze

EUROVISION SONG CONTEST

What is it that compels one hundred million people or more across Europe and the world to tune in their televisions to the annual *Eurovision Song Contest*? Is it the assurance of seeing laughably bad music and onstage gimmicks? Or is it a resounding sense of national pride and a desire to see their homeland take the prize? Every year since 1956, participating countries across Europe have sent a performer to the *Eurovision Song Contest* to play one song. Each country then votes for what they think is the best song by another contender (a country can't vote for itself). It sounds simple, but conspiracy theories abound about votes being motivated more by politics than the quality of the music.

"Waterloo" by ABBA won in 1974, which launched the band to fame. One lucky break occurred in 1994 when Irishman Michael Flatley, who had an act called Riverdance, was booked as the intermission entertainment. His performance led him to the big time. The UK so far has had five winners: Sandie Shaw, "Puppet on a String" (1967); Lulu,

"Boom Bang-a-Bang" (1969); Brotherhood of Man, "Save Your Kisses for Me" (1976); Bucks Fizz, "Making Up Your Mind" (1981); and Katrina and the Waves, "Love Shine a Light" (1997). In the history of the contest, Ireland has had the most winners, and Portugal is still waiting for its moment in the spotlight.

MUSIC AWARDS

There are two main music awards in the UK: the Brits and the Nationwide Mercury Prize, usually known just as the Mercury Prize. The Brits are the music industry's awards and, like the Grammys, are largely an exercise in self-congratulation, usually being awarded to performers that no self-respecting music snob would be caught dead listening to.

The Mercury Prize was founded to try and remedy this by celebrating the best British or Irish album of the past year, with regard only to the strength of the music. To some extent it succeeds: With the benefit of hindsight one can see that the judges really did select albums that have stood the test of time, and the prize has helped promote the sales of little-known artists. On another level, the prize is too ambitious. The short-listed albums for the prize always cover such an extremity of styles, from classical to folk to electronica, that, as 2005 winner Antony said, it becomes "a contest between an orange and a spaceship and a potted plant and a spoon."

NATIONWIDE MERCURY PRIZE WINNERS

Band	Winning Album
1992 Primal Scream	Screamadelica
1993 Suede	Suede
1994 M People	Elegant Slumming
1995 Portishead	Dummy
1996 Pulp	Different Class
1997 Roni Size and Reprazent	New Forms
1998 Gomez	Bring It On
1999 Talvin Singh	OK
2000 Badly Drawn Boy	The Hour of Bewilderbeast
2001 P. J. Harvey	Stories from the City, Stories from the Sea
2002 Ms. Dynamite	A Little Deeper
2003 Dizzee Rascal	Boy in Da Corner
2004 Franz Ferdinand	Franz Ferdinand
2005 Antony and the Johnsons	I Am a Bird Now
2006 Arctic Monkeys	Whatever People Say I Am, That's What I'm Not
2007 Klaxons	Myths of the Near Future
2008 Elbow	The Seldom Seen Kid

Glastonbury is a music festival that has been held on Michael Eavis's Worthy Farm in southwest England since the early 1970s. The three-day event, one of the world's largest festivals, takes place in late June and features poetry, theater, comedy, plenty of drugs, and some of the biggest names in indie music. While Glastonbury might be fun, it's not always fun in the sun. Torrential rain has plagued the festival in recent years, making mud the common denominator and wellies a must-have accessory. The record attendance so far has been about 177,000 people, many of whom camp out in the fields.

Groovy Times and Famous Scenes

The Scene	Mods
Where	London and Brighton.
Golden Age	Early to mid-1960s with a sizable revival in the late 1970s.
The Music	The Small Faces, the Who, the Kinks, American R & B.
The Look	Vespa motor scooters, tailored continental suits, Fred Perry tennis shirts.
Check Out	Colin MacInnes's novel *Absolute Beginners,* the Who's *My Generation,* and anything by the Small Faces; the 1979 film *Quadrophenia* inspired the revival.

The Scene	Swinging London
Where	London, and in particular Carnaby Street and Chelsea's King's Road.
Golden Age	Mid- to late 1960s.
The Music	The Beatles, the Stones, and the whole British Invasion crowd.
The Look	Developing from the drainpipe trousers and Chelsea boots of the mods to the Edwardian flair of the psychedelic scene; Mary Quant designed the clothes, Twiggy modeled them, and David Bailey took the pictures.
Check Out	The Beatles' *Sgt. Pepper's Lonely Hearts Club Band* LP and Michelangelo Antonioni's movie *Blowup.*

The Scene	British Folkies
Where	Scottish Highlands and the West Country.
Golden Age	Late 1960s and early 1970s.
The Music	Donovan, Pentangle, Van Morrison, Fairport Convention, Steeleye Span, and Nick Drake.
The Look	Middle-class suburbanites attempting to pass themselves off as farmers from the past.
Check Out	Van Morrison's *Astral Weeks, Led Zeppelin III,* and Fairport Convention's *Liege and Lief* LPs.

The Scene	Glam
Where	London.
Golden Age	Early 1970s.
The Music	T. Rex, Bowie, Roxy Music, Gary Glitter, and Slade.
The Look	Futuristic androgynous kitsch: platform shoes, eyeliner, glitter, boas, and satin shirts, all purveyed by the legendary Biba boutique of Kensington High Street.
Check Out	*The Rocky Horror Picture Show,* T. Rex's *Main Man,* and David Bowie's *Ziggy Stardust* LPs.

The Scene	Punk
Where	London, Manchester, and other cities.
Golden Age	Mid- to late 1970s.
The Music	Sex Pistols, the Clash, the Jam, the Damned, and the Buzz-cocks.
The Look	Vivienne Westwood crafted the aesthetic, as sold at Malcolm McLaren's shop Sex on the King's Road.
Check Out	Sex Pistols' *Never Mind the Bollocks* LP and the Clash's eponymous first album (UK edition); some so-so movies, like *The Great Rock 'n' Roll Swindle* and *Breaking Glass*.

The Scene	New Romantic
Where	London, Sheffield, Birmingham, and other cities. The gloomier the city, the more fabulous the look.
Golden Age	Early 1980s.
The Music	Duran Duran, Adam and the Ants, Spandau Ballet, Visage, and Culture Club.
The Look	Space-age Glam from designers Zandra Rhodes and Vivienne Westwood and labels such as Boy and Fiorucci.
Check Out	Visage's "Fade to Gray" single; Human League's *Dare* and Duran Duran's *Rio* LPs.

The Scene	Goth
Where	Anywhere the sun doesn't shine.
Golden Age	Early to mid-1980s.
The Music	Siouxsie and the Banshees, the Cure, Bauhaus, and Sisters of Mercy.
The Look	Funereal black clothing, often fetishist or neo-Victorian, with too much make-up.
Check Out	Bauhaus' "Bela Lugosi's Dead" single; Siouxsie and the Banshees' *Juju* and the Cure's *The Head on the Door* LPs.

The Scene	Acid House (aka Rave)
Where	An abandoned warehouse or empty field somewhere.
Golden Age	Late 1980s to early 1990s.
The Music	KLF, 808 State, S'Express, the Shamen, the Prodigy.
The Look	Anything with a big yellow smiley face on it; saucer-wide eyes (a side effect of the drug Ecstasy).
Check Out	The KLF's *White Room* album, Adamski and Seal's dance-floor hit "Killer," and the Chemical Brothers' album *Exit Planet Dust*.

The Scene	Madchester
Where	Manchester, with the Hacienda nightclub as its epicenter.
Golden Age	Late 1980s to early 1990s.
The Music	The Stone Roses, Happy Mondays, Charlatans, and Inspiral Carpets.
The Look	Baggy trousers and floppy sun hats from Manchester labels Joe Bloggs and Gio-Goi; Reebok tennis shoes.
Check Out	Stone Roses' eponymous first album, Happy Mondays' *Pills 'n' Thrills and Bellyaches* album; Michael Winterbottom's 2002 film *24 Hour Party People* wonderfully summarized the movement.

The Scene	Trip Hop
Where	Bristol.
Golden Age	Mid- to late 1990s.
The Music	Massive Attack, Portishead, and Tricky.
The Look	A little bit hip-hop and a little bit indie, with a splash of reggae.
Check Out	Portishead's *Dummy* and Massive Attack's *Blue Lines* albums.

The Scene	Brit Pop
Where	London, Manchester, and beyond.
Golden Age	1990s to early 2000s.
The Music	Oasis, Blur, Pulp, Ocean Colour Scene, and Elastica.
The Look	Casual clothes by Alexander McQueen, Lonsdale, and Fred Perry, all consciously influenced by 1960s mod culture.
Check Out	Oasis' (*What's the Story*) *Morning Glory?*, Pulp's *Different Class*, and Blur's *Parklife;* artists like Damien Hirst and Marcus Harvey; films such as Danny Boyle's *Trainspotting*.

The Scene	Grime/Dubstep
Where	London and other inner cities.
Golden Age	Mid- to late 2000s.
The Music	Dizzee Rascal, Sway, Roll Deep, and Lady Sovereign.
The Look	Baseball caps, baggy T-shirts, hoodies: essentially an imitation of American hip-hop street style.
Check Out	Skream's "Midnight Request Line," Burial's self-titled album, and Dizzee Rascal's *Maths and English* album.

ART

The Turner Prize has been unrivaled in its continual ability to stir up controversy and attract media attention—an enviable accomplishment for a contemporary art award. Each year, works from the four artists on the short list for the award are put on display at Tate Britain to inevitable howls of outrage by *Daily Mail* readers and fawning, frequently uncritical praise from the modern art intelligentsia. To be eligible, artists must be under fifty and living or working in Britain. The judges are drawn from art critics, museum curators, and gallery directors. Past winners have included Howard Hodgkin (1985), Gilbert and George (1986), Richard Long (1989), Anish Kapoor (1991), Rachel Whiteread (1993), Damien Hirst (1995), Keith Tyson (2002), and Tomma Abts (2006).

A FEW MAJOR BRITISH ARTISTS

1500s and 1600s
Hans Holbein the Younger (1497?–1543) Originally German
but flourished in England

Nicholas Hilliard (1547–1619)

Sir Peter Lely (1618–80) Originally German

1700s
William Hogarth (1697–1764)
Sir Joshua Reynolds (1723–92)
George Stubbs (1724–1806)
Thomas Gainsborough (1727–88)
George Romney (1734–1802)
Sir Henry Raeburn (1756–1823)
William Blake (1757–1827)

1800s

J. M. W. Turner (1775–1851)

John Constable (1776–1837)

Sir Edwin Landseer (1802–73)

Dante Gabriel Rossetti (1828–82)

Sir John Everett Millais, Bt. (1829–96)

William Morris (1834–96)

1900s

Sir Stanley Spencer (1891–1959)

Henry Moore (1898–1986)

Dame Barbara Hepworth (1903–75)

Francis Bacon (1909–92)

TODAY

Bridget Riley (b. 1931)

Sir Howard Hodgkin (b. 1932)

Sir Peter Blake (b. 1932)

David Hockney (b. 1937)

Dinos Chapman (b. 1962) and Jake Chapman (b. 1966)

Rachel Whiteread (b. 1963)

Tracey Emin (b. 1963)

Damien Hirst (b. 1965)

Sam Taylor-Wood (b. 1967)

Chris Ofili (b. 1968)

TEN FAMOUS BRITISH PAINTINGS

- *The Wilton Diptych,* artist unknown, ca. 1395
- *Portrait of Henry VIII* by Hans Holbein the Younger, ca. 1537
- *A Rake's Progress* by William Hogarth, ca. 1733
- *Reverend Robert Walker Skating on Duddingston Loch* by Sir Henry Raeburn, ca. 1795
- *Newton* by William Blake, ca. 1805
- *The Hay Wain* by John Constable, 1821
- *The Fighting Temeraire* by J. M. W. Turner, 1838
- *The Last of England* by Ford Madox Brown, 1855
- *Christ Preaching at Cookham Regatta* by Stanley Spencer, 1959
- *Mr. and Mrs. Clark and Percy* by David Hockney, 1970–71

BRITISH HUMOR

It's easy to agree that Britain's distinctive humor is one of the nation's defining features. What's more difficult is to explain exactly what British humor is. Taking a stab at it, we'll say that compared to American humor, it's more biting, absurd, and self-deprecating. British humor has more teasing and ridicule and a clear penchant for camp.

There's always been an audience for British humor in the US, from Monty Python and Benny Hill to *Are You Being Served?* In more recent years, the shows *The Office, Absolutely Fabulous,* and *Mr. Bean,* as well as the comics Ricky Gervais, Eddie Izzard, and Sacha Baron Cohen (of Ali G. and Borat fame) have made it across the Atlantic. Here are some British comic gems you may be less familiar with.

Carry On Movies

These are a series of low-budget, and lowbrow, comedic films characterized by slapstick, double entendres, innuendo, camp, and sexual jokes. They are typical examples of classic British humor and started in 1958 with *Carry On Sergeant*. Other titles include *Carry On Nurse, Carry On England,* and *Carry On Cowboy.* New titles were produced at the rate of one or more a year until 1978; since then only a couple have appeared. So iconic are they that the Royal Mail issued stamps in 2008 featuring some of the old film posters.

Monty Python

They jumped the pond in a big way, but no British comedy section would be complete without mention of Monty Python. In 1969, John Cleese, Graham Chapman, Terry Gilliam (an American), Eric Idle, Terry Jones, and Michael Palin created *Monty Python's Flying Circus* for television. Their seminal show became popular in America as well as the UK. Movies included *Monty Python and the Holy Grail* (1975), *Life of Brian* (1979), and *Monty Python's The Meaning of Life* (1983).

Lenny Henry

The first mainstream black comic in Britain, Lenny Henry, whose family is from the West Indies, got his start by winning a celebrity-judged talent show in 1975 at the age of sixteen. He appeared on *Tiswas,* a children's TV show, on *The Fosters* in 1976–77 (based on the US sitcom *Good Times,* it was the first predominantly black British sitcom), and on *Three of a Kind,* with Tracey Ullman. The hugely popular *Lenny Henry Show* started on the BBC in 1984 as a sketch comedy show building on Henry's stand-up background. Some of his more memorable characters are Delbert Wilkins, a Brixton "wide boy" (wheeler and dealer); Theophilus P. Wildebeeste, a Barry White–esque soul singer and lover of women; and Grandpa Deakus, a West Indian dispenser of clichéd profundity. In 1989, Henry put out Britain's first stand-up comedy film *Lenny Henry Live and Unleashed.*

Stephen Fry and Hugh Laurie

Part of the set that met at Cambridge University's famous Footlights theater group, which included Emma Thompson and Tony Slattery,

Stephen Fry and Hugh Laurie started working together as a team while still at university in the early 1980s. Their comedy sketch show *A Little Bit of Fry and Laurie* was very successful, running on the BBC from 1989 to 1995. The two also made appearances on the seminal comedy *Black-adder*. Arguably their best collaboration was *Jeeves and Wooster,* in which Hugh Laurie played the bumbling toff Bertie Wooster to Fry's straight-man valet, Jeeves, in the dramatization of P. G. Wodehouse's Jeeves stories. The two work together only sporadically now but both are active individually. Stephen Fry has written novels, plays, and screenplays and just finished hosting a comedy panel program called *QI*. Hugh Laurie has been equally prolific and has become well known to American audiences through his starring role in the US medical drama *House*.

Steve Coogan

This English comedian first found fame with his character Alan Partridge, a fictional radio and TV host who is awkward, insecure, smug, frumpy, status conscious, and unlikable, and has terrible fashion sense. When asked about his favorite band, Alan answers, "Wings, the band the Beatles could have been." As Partridge, Coogan appeared on various radio and television shows and got his own show in the mid-1990s, *Knowing Me, Knowing You . . . with Alan Partridge,* then later *I'm Alan Partridge.* Steve Coogan also does stand-up comedy and has appeared in numerous movies, including *24 Hour Party People* and *Hamlet 2.*

Dawn French and Jennifer Saunders

It is safe to say that French and Saunders, creators of six series between 1987 and 2004, a retrospective series in 2007, and myriad Christmas specials, are the most popular female comedy duo in British entertainment history. Their sketches skewer and satirize celebrities, cinema, and celebrity culture. The two work together now only on the specials, devoting the bulk of their energies to their busy solo careers. Jennifer Saunders will be familiar to many Americans through writing and costarring in the Emmy-winning sitcom *Absolutely Fabulous* (she's Edina). Dawn French starred in the BBC sitcoms *The Vicar of Dibley* and

Jam and Jerusalem and is married to the comedian Lenny Henry (see page 112).

Catherine Tate

She's been called "the catchphrase queen" as just about every one of the vast array of characters she plays in the sketches on her show, *The Catherine Tate Show,* has their own oft-repeated identifying line. The first series began in 2004 and since then such lines as "Am I bovvered?" as said by the yobbish teenager Lauren Cooper, and "How very dare you?" as exclaimed by the repressed homosexual Derek Faye, have entered the British phrase book. All of these characters are played by Tate herself, with guest stars from Tony Blair to George Michael pitching in. In 2008, she became costar of the long-running science-fiction series *Dr. Who.*

THE BRITISH FIND MEN IN DRAG TO BE UNCEASINGLY HILARIOUS

Dame Edna Everage, Danny La Rue, and Lily Savage are popular female impersonators.

PANTOMIME

Foreigners are frequently startled to find out just how camp the British are. It's hard to overestimate the profound joy they derive from corny double entendres, cross-dressing, slapstick humor, and old queens. With incredible ingenuity, they've also somehow managed to mix all these things together and create a family-friendly national institution: panto. To Americans, the word "pantomime" conjures up images of mimes. The British pantomime has nothing to do with this. British panto is farce, combining the comedy style of the Italian commedia dell'arte and the exuberance of a nineteenth-century British musical hall.

Pantos appear in theaters across the land around Christmas, coinciding with school vacations—not that the story lines have anything to do with Christmas. They are usually drawn from folktales, with Cinderella, Aladdin, Jack and the Beanstalk, and folklore hero Dick Whittington all perennial favorites. At the heart of every pantomime is the dame, a kindly elder woman's role, such as Jack's mother or the Widow Twankey in Aladdin, usually played by a very effeminate or openly gay man. The pantomime dame tends to be the star attraction and always makes the grandest, most flamboyant entrance. TV actors, reality series stars, and B-list celebs regularly tread the boards during panto season.

THE TELLY

The BBC (British Broadcasting Corporation)—affectionately nicknamed "the Beeb" or "Auntie"—began broadcasting on the radio in 1922 and on television in 1936. Television broadcasts were suspended in 1939 for the duration of World War II. When they resumed in 1946, there was some catching up to do. Television in Britain got its big break on June 2, 1953, when approximately twenty million viewers crowded around what TV sets there were to watch Queen Elizabeth's coronation.

In 1955, ITV (Independent Television) arrived to give the BBC some competition, followed in 1964 by BBC2, giving the British viewing public the staggering choice of three whole television channels to enjoy until the launch of Channel 4 in 1982.

Unlike the other channels on British television and radio, there is no advertising on the BBC. But those who immediately think of PBS and their tiresome phone-a-thons to raise money need not fear. Rather, in Britain, the owner of a television must pay an annual license fee, which in 2009 was £139.50 for a color TV and £47 for a black-and-white set. The fee is half-price for people who are over seventy-four or blind. Needless to say, grumbles and complaints about the licensing fee (which everyone with a television must pay no matter what they watch) and the programming the BBC offers are common. Over time, the BBC's television channels have expanded to include BBC Three, BBC Four, BBC News, BBC Parliament, and CBBC (for kids).

In contrast, ITV was supported by advertising from its inception. Originally a consortium of four private companies producing programming—Granada, ATV, ABC, and Rediffusion—there are now a number of ITV channels, including ITV1, ITV2, ITV3, and ITV4.

In the 1990s, satellite TV arrived and is now very popular. Rupert Murdoch's British Sky Broadcasting, generally known as Sky, dominates, and broadcasts a whole range of channels. The late 1990s also saw the arrival of another terrestrial channel, originally called Channel 5 but later rebranded to the simpler Five. Both Five and Channel 4 have add-on digital channels, such as MoreFour, FilmFour, and Five US, giving UK viewers today a breadth of viewing options similar to those in the US.

THE PERIOD DRAMA

What is it about period dramas that the British love so much? Perhaps the bonnets and braces (suspenders) that the characters wear? Whatever it is, it's clear that the British love a good historical drama, and for proof just take a look at what's on TV—recent broadcasts include adaptations of *A Room with a View, Mansfield Park, Sense and Sensibility,* and *Little Dorrit.* These programs may be popular simply because they are based on really good books. Then again, it might be a sense of nostalgia for a time when Britain was still "Great."

SEMINAL SHOWS

In the US, certain television programs such as *The Brady Bunch, The Tonight Show Starring Johnny Carson,* and *Seinfeld* have become part of the cultural fabric. Here are some television shows that have done the same in the UK.

Doctor Who

Traveling though time, space, and the farther reaches of the BBC's costume department, *Doctor Who* occupies a place in the British psyche akin to that of *Star Trek* to American viewers. Since 1963, the doctor and his leggy assistants have crisscrossed dimensions of space and time fighting evil in the TARDIS, an interstellar vehicle cunningly disguised as a 1950s police department phone booth. The TARDIS is notable for looking small (like a phone booth) from the outside, but actually being spacious on the inside.

Ten different actors played the doctor over twenty-six television seasons, the plot line cunningly allowing the doctor to periodically transform his appearance at the command of that shadowy, unseen force, the BBC's contracts department. The show was cancelled in 1989, only to return with great fanfare in 2005. Over the decades, Doctor Who has faced down actors clad in rubber, fur, metal, and whatever else was within reach of the BBC's costume budget. His greatest foes, though, were the Daleks, a race of mutant robots, who, to the uninitiated, might be mistaken for oversized salt and pepper shakers on wheels and whose diabolical intent was summed up in their battle cry: "Exterminate!"

The show is known for its pioneering use of electronic music and in 2006 won the BAFTA award for best drama series. *Doctor Who* spin-offs include *Torchwood* and *The Sarah Jane Adventures*. With future series and Christmas specials slated for production, *Doctor Who* looks like it's going to keep moving forward through time, space, and multiple dimensions.

Top of the Pops

Required Thursday-evening viewing for generations of teenage music fans, *Top of the Pops,* or *TOTP,* was the classic music program for most of its forty-two-year run. There may have been more innovative predecessors, like *Ready, Steady, Go!* back in the 1960s, or cooler rivals, such as *The Tube* in the 1980s or the current *Later . . . with Jools Holland,* but *TOTP*'s weekly rundown of the charts kept it always of the moment—

that is, until the modern downloading era began and the charts ceased to mean anything. *Top of the Pops* was finally canned in the summer of 2006. Hosted by BBC radio DJs, the show counted down to the week's number one single, with bands along the way performing in the studio or in music videos. Every episode culminated in the number one song, however awful it might be (except for Jane Birkin and Serge Gainsbourg's 1969 ode to heavy-breathing love, "Je T'Aime . . . Moi Non Plus," and Frankie Goes to Hollywood's 1984 smash "Relax," which were both banned by the BBC despite making it to number one).

Dad's Army

During World War II, men who were too old or too young for active duty were asked to join the Home Guard for local defense. In *Dad's Army,* the mostly elderly men of the fictional village of Walmington-on-Sea on the south coast of England step up for duty, to serve king and comedy. Led by pompous bank manager Captain George Mainwaring, the platoon is a mix of the incompetent and the incontinent. *Dad's Army* ran on the BBC from 1968 to 1977 and was made into a full-length movie in 1971.

Blackadder

To Americans familiar with the comedian Rowan Atkinson only through his annoying Mr. Bean character, it will come as something of a surprise to hear British people of otherwise seemingly good taste sing his praises. The reason? *Blackadder.* This ingenious BBC comedy of the 1980s charted the escapades of various members of the Blackadder family, as played by Atkinson, across four series and four and a half centuries of history. These Blackadders included Prince Edmund Blackadder at the end of the Middle Ages; Edmund, Lord Blackadder, at the court of Elizabeth I; Edmund Blackadder, Esq., serving as butler to the idiotic Prince Regent, son of George III; and Captain Blackadder in the trenches of the western front of World War I. Each Blackadder has a not-so-intelligent and much-abused sidekick named Baldrick who serves as the hero's coconspirator.

Only Fools and Horses

When the BBC ran a national poll in 2004 asking the people of Britain to name the country's greatest sitcom of all time, *Only Fools and Horses* won decisively (though *Blackadder* came in at number two). The East London market trader Derek "Del Boy" Trotter, played by David Jason, with his witless, much younger brother, Rodney, played by Nicholas Lyndhurst, acting as sidekick, embodied the much beloved archetypal British character of the cheeky, "duckin' and divin' " wheeler and dealer. Seven series of the show ran between 1981 and 1991, though Christmas specials and one-off episodes have kept the boys from Peckham in the public eye.

Little Britain

It might not be subtle or sophisticated, but it is enormously popular. The recurring characters in the sketch-comedy series *Little Britain* mock all the stereotypes of modern Britain. Starting on BBC radio but soon switching over to television, the duo of Matt Lucas and David Walliams, who write and star in the series, have made their creation one of the most popular comedies of the 2000s. Teenage delinquent Vicky Pollard, moral guardians Maggie and Judy, and Welsh "homosexualist" Daffyd all make fools of themselves, to the public's acclaim and, frequently, the critics' offense. In 2007, Lucas and Walliams switched their focus to producing the American spin-off *Little Britain USA* for HBO.

REALITY MADNESS

Like the US, the UK has had an explosion of reality television shows. Many US programs, in fact, originated in the UK. Some British reality TV highlights:

• *Big Brother,* in which a group of people live under continuous observation, has gained cult status in the UK with contestants filling the pages of the tabloids.

- The British show *Strictly Come Dancing* was reinvented for an American audience as *Dancing with the Stars.*
- *The Apprentice* has a British edition with the business mogul Sir Alan Sugar.
- The British show *Pop Idol* came over to the US as *American Idol.*
- *The X Factor* is a talent show similar to *America's Got Talent, Britain's Got Talent,* and *American Idol.*
- *I'm a Celebrity . . . Get Me Out of Here!* follows a group of celebrities as they navigate challenges in the jungle, far from their assistants.

SOAP OPERAS

A few enduring and much-loved soap operas have become ingrained in British culture. The major difference between soap operas in the US and those in the UK is that US soap operas tend to glamorize upper-class life whereas British soaps focus on the working-class. Think of *Dynasty, Falcon Crest,* and other such aspirational shows in the US versus these British classics:

Affectionately known as *Corrie* or *The Street,* **Coronation Street** is the longest running television soap opera in Britain; it first aired in 1960. In four episodes per week, we follow the trials and tribulations of the residents of Coronation Street in the fictional town of Weathersfield, near Manchester in northwestern England.

Like all good British soap operas, much of the drama centers on a pub, the Rovers Return, where the pints flow and the plot thickens. Some of *Coronation Street*'s best-known characters are Bet Lynch, who wore flamboyant earrings and hopped from man to man, and Hilda Ogden, who worked as a cleaner at the Rovers Return and wore her trademark curlers and headscarf.

EastEnders has been one of the most popular British television shows since it began in 1985. Chronicling the lives of ordinary working-class families living in the fictional borough of Walford in East London,

EastEnders has seen its characters deal with murder, rape, drug addiction, domestic violence, AIDS, cancer, mental illness, and homophobia, among other real-life tragedies.

Once again, the plotlines orbit around the local pub, the Queen Victoria (known to its regulars as "the Queen Vic"). The episodes weave around the members of various families in the community, including the Beales, the Fowlers, the Watts, the Mitchells, the Slaters, and the Brannings.

Emmerdale, originally called *Emmerdale Farm,* is the rural alternative to *EastEnders* and *Coronation Street* and has been running on ITV since 1972. Set in the fictional village of Emmerdale (originally called Beckindale) in West Yorkshire in northern England, the plot revolves around the Sugdens, a farming family. Needless to say, there is a pub, the Woolpack, where plots unfurl and characters scheme.

CHILDREN'S TELEVISION

Most British people won't know about *The Electric Company, Zoom, Mister Rogers' Neighborhood,* or *The Mickey Mouse Club* but will recall the following television programs from their youth.

Blue Peter

Few things are duller than "educational" television, though for fifty years *Blue Peter* has entertained the children of Britain with an endless string of activities, charity appeals, and studio "pet" animals. The show is hosted by groups of overenthusiastic twenty-somethings, periodically refreshed, Menudo-like, with newer, youthful faces. Twice-weekly broadcasts lead the youth of the UK through such craft projects as building a "luxury swing hammock" for dolls out of coat hangers and a shoe box. And then there are the animals. The idea was that the children of the nation would all get to share in the joys of owning a pet together. Over the years, this menagerie has included a host of dogs, cats, and tortoises.

The Basil Brush Show

A small fox puppet with a big personality and a rather posh accent, Basil Brush was created in 1963 by Peter Firmin and, after appearing on various shows, got his own, *The Basil Brush Show,* on BBC in 1970. Basil's distinctive laugh, catchphrase "Boom Boom!" after a joke, and somewhat corny humor have captured the imaginations of British kids (and adults, too). Basil always had a straight man—Mr. Roy and Mr. Derek were two—who set up the jokes and never cracked a smile amid all the hilarity. Basil also put out an album titled *Boom Boom It's Basil Brush,* and had his television show resurrected in 2002. Not bad for a fox puppet with no legs and a limited range of motion.

The Magic Roundabout

British children of the 1960s, '70s, and '90s (when a whole horde of never-before-shown episodes were broadcast on Channel 4) didn't need drugs to go on psychedelic trips. They simply watched *The Magic Roundabout.* This cult program chronicled, in five-minute episodes, the bizarre adventures of characters such as Dougal, a shaggy dog; Ermintrude, a bossy cow; and Dylan, a guitar-strumming, seemingly stoned rabbit. *The Magic Roundabout* was originally a French creation, but with the original plot lines and narration of Eric Thompson, father of the actress Emma Thompson, the BBC version far outshone the original.

The Wombles

The Wombles are fluffy rodents with pointy noses who live in a burrow under Wimbledon Common. Overseen by the patriarch Great Uncle Bulgaria, they venture out to pick up litter, which they then recycle. The original program ran for just two seasons in the mid-1970s but proved so iconic, and their environmental message so resonant, that it spawned a legacy of records, television specials, and a feature-length film before returning to television in the late 1990s for a whole new generation.

TELEVISION AND RADIO LEGENDS

You may not have heard of them, but in the UK these are well-known names.

Cilla Black

As hat-check girl and occasional performer at Liverpool's famous Cavern Club in the early 1960s, Cilla Black can truly be said to have been in the right place at the right time. Through the efforts of John Lennon, she was signed up as a singer by Beatles manager Brian Epstein. Her first hit, a version of Burt Bacharach's "Anyone Who Had a Heart," became the bestselling single ever by a woman in England to that point. Cilla went on to become the second bestselling musical act out of Liverpool in the 1960s (after you-know-who).

In 1968, the BBC gave her a TV variety show called *Cilla,* followed by the show that has come to define her, *Blind Date,* which made her reportedly the highest paid woman on British television.

John Peel

The longest serving DJ on BBC Radio 1, John Peel (1939–2004) was a legend in the UK known for championing new music and giving early exposure to the likes of Marc Bolan (T. Rex), David Bowie, Blur, and the Smiths. Originally from the Liverpool area, he joined BBC Radio 1 at its launch in 1967. During "Peel sessions," he scheduled studio time for all sorts of cutting-edge artists (including an early session in 1989 by Nirvana). He's credited with giving exposure to punk, hip-hop, and reggae before they were mainstream. Famously, his favorite song was "Teenage Kicks" by the Undertones and his favorite band was the Fall.

Terry Wogan

A beloved legend of light entertainment, Terry Wogan has been a major presence over the British radio and television airwaves since the 1970s. His first regular show on BBC Radio was *Midday Spin.* His BBC Radio 2 program *Wake Up to Wogan* has approximately eight million listeners.

Born in Limerick, Ireland, Wogan affectionately calls his listeners "TOGs," which stands for Terry's Old Geezers or Gals. Wogan received an honorary knighthood in 2005 and has since become a British citizen, so he can now be called Sir Terry Wogan.

Melvyn Bragg

Britain's high-culture guru Melvyn Bragg (or, properly, Lord Bragg of Wigton, after he was made a peer in 1998) is a prolific writer and presenter for television and radio. His highbrow documentaries and series include *12 Books That Changed the World* and *Melvyn Bragg's Travels in Written Britain*. Much of his work focuses on the different regions of Britain. Originally from working-class roots in Cumbria in northern England, he's been a host of *The South Bank Show* for London Weekend Television since 1978 and has written many novels and nonfiction books, including a series of autobiographical novels titled *The Soldier's Return* (1999), *A Son of War* (2001), *Crossing the Lines* (2003), and *Remember Me . . .* (2008). The huge quantity, and high quality, of his work in television, radio, and print have made him one of the nation's most beloved public intellectuals.

Chris Evans

An example of where a maverick with ambition can go, ginger-haired Chris Evans went from being a regular radio DJ to a high-profile media mogul. Born in 1966 into a working-class family in northwestern England, he made a name for himself with his irreverent interviewing style as one of the original presenters on the popular television show *The Big Breakfast* on Channel 4 in 1992. He formed Ginger Productions in 1993, which created the television show *Don't Forget Your Toothbrush*. This show became a big hit in the UK and was sold to stations around the world. Then the moguling began. In 1997, his Ginger Media Group purchased Virgin Radio from Richard Branson for £85 million; three years later he sold his company to the Scottish Media Group for £225 million, personally earning him about £75 million. Not bad for a guy whose bios start with how he was bullied in school and dropped out at age sixteen.

Ant and Dec

Television hosts Anthony McPartlin and Declan Donnelly, both from Newcastle ("Geordies"), met in their early teens while acting on the children's television show *Byker Grove*. After releasing their hit song "Let's Get Ready to Rumble" and a string of other singles, they got their own TV show called *The Ant and Dec Show,* followed by *Ant and Dec Unzipped* on Channel 4. Next came the award-winning *SM:TV Live* and *CD:UK,* which was cohosted by Cat Deeley. Then they moved to weekend prime time with *Ant and Dec's Saturday Night Takeaway,* featuring celebrity guests, interviews, and musical numbers. They're regular presenters on hit shows such as *I'm a Celebrity . . . Get Me Out of Here!, Britain's Got Talent,* and *Pop Idol.*

BAFTA

The British Academy of Film and Television Arts (BAFTA) has held annual award ceremonies, usually in February, for achievement in film since 1947. The BAFTA television awards are held separately, usually in April or May. BAFTA is similar to the Academy of Motion Picture Arts and Sciences, which hosts the Oscars each spring.

BRITISH FILM AND STAGE

SOME LEGENDARY BRITISH ACTORS

Sir John Gielgud (1904–2000). *Murder on the Orient Express* (1974); *Arthur* (1981); *Prospero's Books* (1991).

Sir Laurence Olivier (1907–89). *Wuthering Heights* (1939); *Henry V* (1944); *Hamlet* (1948); *Richard III* (1955); *Sleuth* (1972); *Marathon Man* (1976).

Sir Michael Redgrave (1908–85). (Father of Vanessa and Lynn Redgrave.) *The Lady Vanishes* (1938); *The Browning Version* (1951); *Goodbye, Mr. Chips* (1969); *Nicholas and Alexandra* (1971).

Sir Alec Guinness (1914–2000). *Kind Hearts and Coronets* (1949); *The Lavender Hill Mob* (1951); *The Bridge on the River Kwai* (1957); *Lawrence of Arabia* (1962); *Star Wars* (1977); *A Passage to India* (1984).

Peter Sellers (1925–80). *The Mouse That Roared* (1959); *Lolita* (1962); *The Pink Panther* (1963); *Dr. Strangelove* (1964); *Being There* (1979).

Sir Sean Connery (b. 1930). James Bond films in the 1960s; *Marnie* (1964); *The Untouchables* (1987); *Indiana Jones and the Last Crusade* (1989); *The Hunt for Red October* (1990); *Dragonheart* (1996); *The League of Extraordinary Gentlemen* (2003).

Dame Judi Dench (b. 1934). *A Room with a View* (1985); *A Handful of Dust* (1988); *Mrs. Brown* (1997); *Shakespeare in Love* (1998); *Iris* (2001); *Casino Royale* (2006); *Notes on a Scandal* (2006).

Dame Maggie Smith (b. 1934). *The Prime of Miss Jean Brodie* (1969); *Death on the Nile* (1978); *Clash of the Titans* (1981); *A Room with a View* (1985); the Harry Potter films.

Helen Mirren (b. 1945). *Cal* (1984); *White Nights* (1985); *The Mosquito Coast* (1986); *The Cook, the Thief, His Wife, and Her Lover* (1989); *Gosford Park* (2001); *Calendar Girls* (2003); *The Queen* (2006).

RADIO

In the UK there is a great history of radio documentary and drama. Legendary radio programs of the UK include:

Desert Island Discs

One of the longest running radio shows around, *Desert Island Discs* is a weekly program on BBC Radio 4 that was created in 1942 by Roy Plomley. Each week a guest says what eight songs, one book, and one inanimate luxury item he or she would bring if stranded on a desert island (the Bible and the complete works of Shakespeare are already on the island). Guests reveal themselves by talking about their choices.

Roy Plomley hosted the show until his death in 1985. Since then it's been hosted by Michael Parkinson, Sue Lawley, and Kirsty Young. Some guests on *Desert Island Discs* and their choices:

Nick Hornby, author

Songs: "Kitty's Back" by Bruce Springsteen
"You Wear It Well" by Rod Stewart
"Complainte Pour Ste Catherine" by Kate and Anna McGarrigle
"The Love You Save" by Jackson Five
"Fatou Yo" by Touré Kunda
"Night Ride Home" by Joni Mitchell
"My Heart Is the Bums on the Street" by Marah
"Going Back to Cali" by LL Cool J
Book: *Barnaby Rudge* by Charles Dickens
Luxury: iPod

David Cameron, leader of the Conservative Party

Songs: "Tangled Up In Blue" by Bob Dylan
"Ernie" by Benny Hill
"Wish You Were Here" by Pink Floyd
"On Wings of Song" by Kiri Te Kanawa and the
    Utah Symphony Orchestra
"Fake Plastic Trees" by Radiohead
"This Charming Man" by the Smiths
"Perfect Circle" by R.E.M
"All These Things That I've Done" by the Killers
Book: *The River Cottage Cookbook*
    by Hugh Fearnley-Whittingstall
Luxury: A crate of Scottish whisky

George Michael, musician

Songs: "Love Is a Losing Game" by Amy Winehouse
"Do the Strand" by Roxy Music
"Crazy" by Gnarls Barkley
"Smells Like Teen Spirit" by Nirvana
"Being Boring" by the Pet Shop Boys
"Paper Bag" by Goldfrapp
"Gold Digger" by Kanye West
"Going to Town" by Rufus Wainwright
Book: Any book of short stories by Doris Lessing
Luxury: DB9 car

Simon Cowell, host and producer

Songs: "Mack the Knife" by Bobby Darin
"This Guy's in Love with You" by Herb Alpert
"She" by Charles Aznavour
"Unchained Melody" by the Righteous Brothers
"Danke Schoen" by Wayne Newton
"If You're Not the One" by Daniel Bedingfield
"Summer Wind" by Frank Sinatra
"Mr. Bojangles" by Sammy Davis, Jr.
Book: *Hollywood Wives* by Jackie Collins
Luxury: A mirror

Today

With more than six million listeners a week, *Today* is BBC Radio 4's most popular show. It is a morning news program that has been on the air since 1957. Jack de Manio hosted until the late 1970s, when John Timpson and Brian Redhead took over. In 1986, John Humphreys and Sue MacGregor came on board. Recent hosts include Jim Naughtie, Ed Stourton, Sarah Montague, and Evan Davis. It's comparable to NPR's *All Things Considered*.

The Archers

Debuting in 1950, *The Archers* is the world's longest running radio drama. Airing on BBC Radio 4, the twelve-and-a-half minute episodes follow the lives of the Archers, a rural middle-class family who own and operate Brookfield Farm. Other families are featured in the show, such as the working-class Grundys and the well-to-do Aldridges. *The Archers* takes place in the fictional town of Ambridge, a community in the midlands of England. The episodes (there are six per week with an omnibus edition on Sunday) are recorded in advance but tie in with current events. When necessary, they are rerecorded if a big news story breaks, such as the death of the Queen Mother or the World Trade Center attacks.

In 1955, people around England were stunned when one of the main characters, Grace Archer, was killed in a stable fire while trying to rescue her horse. Recently, some listeners have been outraged by racier story lines, such as the characters' affairs.

FACT OR FICTION?

The British have a perverse love for white musicians who they think sound like black Americans.
Fact. Just look at Van Morrison, Jamiroquai, Amy Winehouse, Simply Red, Tom Jones, and Joss Stone.

British people go to France when they feel like they need some culture and fine dining.
Fiction. They go to France on day trips to load up on cheap booze and cigarettes.

Simon Cowell, the brutally honest judge on American Idol, *is well known in the US, but hardly anyone in the UK has ever heard of him.*
Fiction. Simon Cowell (who is English) is also a major phenomenon in the UK. Through his production company, Syco, he's created and executive produced the shows *American Inventor* and *America's Got Talent,* and has judged the UK version of the globally franchised *Pop Idol, Britain's Got Talent,* and the British hit show *The X Factor.* Before getting into talent shows, he was a successful artist and repertoire consultant in the UK for Sony BMG.

CHAPTER 4

POLITICS AND GOVERNMENT

Loosely following the Roman Republican model, the UK's parliament is a bicameral body, consisting of a lower house, the House of Commons, and an upper house, the House of Lords, with the reigning monarch presiding over both. Or so it goes in theory. In actuality, the queen has zero political power, and at her annual queen's speech to Parliament she simply recites a script provided by the ruling political party.

THE HOUSE OF COMMONS

The House of Commons holds elected members from England, Scotland, Northern Ireland, and Wales. In total there are 646 members of "the Commons," though this number has fluctuated over time. The primary function of the House of Commons is to pass legislation.

The prime minister is the leader of the majority party of the House of Commons and acts as the chief executive of government. When the ruling party in Parliament changes, the prime minister also changes.

General elections, in which people throughout the UK vote for members of the House of Commons (though not directly for a prime minister), are not held on a specific schedule as they are in the US. The prime minister must call a general election within five years of the previous one. There's much less balance in this system than there is in the United States. The party with the most total seats gets both a majority in the House of Commons and also the prime ministership, unlike the US where there can be, for example, a Republican president and a Democratic majority in Congress.

THE HOUSE OF LORDS

"The Lords," as it is usually termed, was until recently dominated by hereditary peers, that is, aristocrats who had inherited their titles and whose best qualification to govern was that some ancestor of theirs had been a hunting buddy of some long-dead king. As the eighteenth-century member Lord Chesterfield said in a speech to the house: "We, my lords, may thank heaven that we have something better than our brains to depend upon."

The past decade has seen major movement toward reforming the Lords, and in 2007 the House of Commons passed a measure calling for the removal of most hereditary peers from the Lords—though their titles will remain intact. Instead, the chamber will seat almost exclusively life peers. There is also a movement in the Labour government to make the House of Lords an elected body, something like the Senate in the US.

Life peers are people to whom the monarch has given, with the government's advice, a peerage that expires on their death. Life peers are exclusively barons. In theory, peerages are given for services to the nation, be they political, cultural, or economic, though Tony Blair has not been the first prime minister to suffer under accusations of trading these titles for money and favors.

Once immensely powerful, the House of Lords has seen its authority dramatically curtailed in the past century. Today it serves mostly as a forum for debate and revision of bills, and as a provider of convenient parking in central London for its members. Its only real legislative power is to delay bills, though its influence can sometimes make or break government proposals.

POLITICAL NAMES AND PLACES

Number 10 Downing Street

Similar to the White House in Washington, this is both the home and the offices of the prime minister. The building, in Westminster, has been used by the prime minister since the 1730s. It is often referred to simply as "Number 10."

Number 11 Downing Street

Right next to Number 10, this is where the chancellor of the exchequer (the treasurer) lives and works. When Tony Blair was prime minister, he swapped residences with Gordon Brown, then the chancellor of the exchequer, because the living quarters at 11 Downing Street are bigger than at Number 10, and the Blairs have four children. This, too, might be referred to simply as "Number 11."

Numbers 9 and 12 Downing Street

These buildings are, alas, not quite as special as numbers 10 and 11, though they hold offices for the staff of the prime minister and the chancellor of the exchequer.

Chequers

This is the country retreat for the prime minister, like the US president's Camp David. About forty miles northwest of London in Buckinghamshire, the thousand-acre estate was privately owned by Lord Lee of Fareham, who donated it to the nation in 1917. The first prime minister to make use of Chequers was David Lloyd George in 1921. Winston Churchill spent time there, in particular during the bombing raids on London in World War II. US presidents and other foreign dignitaries have been regular visitors.

Whitehall

This is the name of a road in Westminster that runs from the Houses of Parliament to Trafalgar Square. It's also the name of the surrounding area, which includes Downing Street and many government ministries. You might see in newspapers, for example, phrases such as "Whitehall spent £100,000" or "Whitehall jobs being slashed." In this case, the name is used to mean the central government.

Like many things in the UK, Whitehall is not a new thing. Henry VIII made Whitehall the central location of government during his reign; Whitehall Palace was Henry VIII's court in the 1530s. That building burned down in the late seventeenth century, but today this street and the surrounding area is still the hub for government buildings and goings-on.

Buckingham Palace

When "Buckingham Palace" says something, it means the monarch's minions and spokespeople.

The Home Office

This is the government department in charge of protecting the people of the UK from crime, terrorism, and antisocial behavior. It oversees all the police in the UK, drug laws, immigration, and threats to national security, from terrorism in particular.

MI5

Officially named the Security Service, MI5 is Britain's domestic intelligence and counterterrorism agency. Formed before World War I to dig out German spies, the agency was originally part of the military—the name by which it is universally known today is derived from the fact that it was section five of military intelligence during World War I. MI5 today is part of the Home Office, though the government did not even acknowledge the existence of this super-secret organization until 1989.

MI6

The adventures of James Bond have made MI6 one of the most famous intelligence agencies in the world. The government now acknowledges the existence of the Secret Intelligence Service (SIS), as MI6 is officially called, but little more—the agency still retains the power to censor media coverage of its activities. MI6 covers foreign intelligence (M15 controls domestic intelligence), and is overseen by the Foreign Office. Like MI5, MI6 was a product of World War I; it was known as section six of military intelligence in the postwar years.

As for the idea, popularized by the James Bond stories, that everyone in MI6 is referred to only by single-letter code names, there is some truth to it. The first head of the organization, Captain Sir Mansfield Cumming, RN, signed himself "C," a habit continued by all his successors.

SAS

The SAS are the "Special Air Service," the British military's crack special forces unit. These are the balaclava-wearing guys who storm hijacked planes and pursue missions deep behind enemy lines. Their famous motto is "Who Dares Wins."

SIS

See MI6.

BRITISH POLITICAL PARTIES

Following the broad rule that the smaller the country, the more political parties there are, Britain has three dominant parties—the Conservative (aka "Tory"), Labour, and Liberal Democrat parties—plus a plethora of regional and special interest ones. Needless to say, the fringe parties tend to be more interesting than the big three. They range from the unpronounceable (the earnest Welsh nationalist Plaid Cymru) to the ridiculous (the Official Monster Raving Loony Party). The existence of this many parties indicates both the seriousness with which the British electorate treats local issues, and the lack of reverence they have for their elected representatives.

POLITICAL PARTY COLORS

In the US we talk about red states and blue states, and everyone knows we're referring to Republican- and Democratic-leaning states. What colors in Britain signify the major political parties?

Conservative = Blue
Labour = Red (the old color of revolutionary socialism)
Liberal Democrats = Gold or yellow

Conservative Party

The Conservative Party, colloquially known as the Tory party, is the major right-wing party. For most of the twentieth century they were the dominant political force. Think of them as the British version of the Republicans, with all the same talk about free trade, low taxes, a strong military, and such. While they're not quite as wrapped up in morals as US conservatives—the whole God thing isn't such an issue in British politics—they're still preachy enough that the nation smiles whenever another Tory member of Parliament (MP) is caught up in some sex scandal or other.

Famous Conservative prime ministers include Maggie Thatcher (1979–90), Harold Macmillan (1957–63), Winston Churchill (1940–45 and 1951–55), and Benjamin Disraeli (1868 and 1874–80).

Labour Party

The Labour Party was formed in the early twentieth century when working-class people became frustrated with the Liberal Party (which has evolved into today's Liberal Democrat Party). Not surprisingly, given its name, the Labour Party was aligned with the trade unions and championed such issues as education and social services. In the 1990s, Tony Blair grabbed the steering wheel, and "New Labour" was born. The old guard may have griped about the abandonment of socialist principles, but by moving the party toward the center and absorbing many of the Conservatives' ideas on finance and spending, Blair initiated the Labour Party's longest run in power. Historically, the Labour Party was well to the left of the American Democrats, but today the comparison is apt. Despite his affinity for photo ops with George W. Bush, Tony Blair's premiership and political style can best be thought of as akin to that of Bill Clinton, with a similar set of strengths, weaknesses, and vanities, albeit without the personal sex scandals. His successor, former chancellor of the exchequer Gordon Brown, unfortunately comes across as a bit too much the dour Scot.

They haven't had as many prime ministers as the Conservatives, but famous Labourites include Prime Minister Tony Blair (1997–2007);

Prime Minister Clement Attlee (1945–51); and Aneurin "Nye" Bevan, MP (1929–60), the political force behind establishing the National Health Service in 1946 and hero of the hard left. Bevan's opinions on political centrism are encapsulated in his famous quote "We know what happens to people who stay in the middle of the road. They get run over."

Liberal Democrat Party

The Lib Dems evolved out of a 1988 merger between the older Liberal Party, successor to the Whigs of yore, and the Social Democrats. (The Social Democrat Party was created in 1981 when a number of supporters of the Labour Party defected over organizational reforms. The last remnants of the Social Democrat Party finally packed up when they received fewer votes than the Official Monster Raving Loony Party candidate in a 1990 by-election.) The Liberal Democrats are the third largest party in the country, usually winning about 20 percent of the popular vote. There is no direct comparison with an American political party. The Lib Dems adhere to a basically progressive, center-left philosophy with a strong environmental stance and a platform whose issues include constitutional reform, European integration, and civil liberties. The Lib Dems have never had a prime minister. The party's leaders have included Paddy Ashdown (or Paddy "Pants-Down" as *The Sun* nicknamed him after he was caught cheating on his wife), Charles Kennedy, and, currently, Nick Clegg. As heirs to the Liberal Party, though, they can claim kinship to such prime ministerial heavy-weights as David Lloyd George (1916–22) and William Gladstone (1868–74, 1880–85, 1886, and 1892–94).

THE WHIGS OF YORE

The Whigs were a political faction of the late seventeenth, eighteenth, and early nineteenth centuries who stood in opposition to the Tories and are the ancestors of the modern Liberal Democrat Party. Their political philosophy shifted over time, but broadly they were the party of the aristocracy, constitutional reformers keen to keep the monarch on a tighter leash, and religious dissenters. Opposed to them, the Tories generally stood for the established Anglican Church, the gentry, and the merchants. While the term "Tory" is applied to today's Conservative Party, the term "Whig" has faded from use.

The Scottish National Party

Universally referred to as the SNP, the Scottish National Party was formed in 1934 from the merger of two other Scottish parties. It is similar in its positions to the Labour Party, though in particular it focuses on gaining recognition for Scotland as an independent nation in the EU. Nationally, they don't pull much weight, usually sending only about half a dozen representatives to Parliament in London. Within Scotland, however, they are a significant force as the second largest party within the Scottish parliament at Holyrood. Like any good nationalist movement, their strength is dissipated by divisions within the movement, which has seen the emergence of competitors, such as the Scottish Green and Scottish Socialist parties.

Much as they might like to claim such heroes of Scottish nationalism as Scottish king Robert the Bruce and William Wallace (of *Braveheart* fame), the modern Scottish independence movement has not produced any politicians of significant stature. The guiding light of the SNP since 1990 has been its on-again off-again leader, Alex Salmond.

Plaid Cymru

Despite a remarkable number of vowels (for the Welsh language) in its name, the Welsh nationalist political party stays true to its linguistic roots by being completely unpronounceable in its Celtic splendor. Try saying something along the lines of "plied kum-roo" and you'd be close. Promoter of all things Welsh, including the Welsh language and recognition of Wales as its own nation within the European Union, Plaid Cymru is the standard bearer of mainstream Welsh nationalism and culture. (There are some crazies on the Welsh nationalist fringe who have expressed their nationalism by burning English people's country houses in Wales.)

Founded in the 1920s, Plaid Cymru won its first seat in Parliament in the 1960s. Today they have three of the forty Welsh seats, their support concentrated in the Welsh-speaking western part of the country. They hold power in the National Assembly for Wales as a junior partner of the Labour Party. While political independence for Wales remains a distant goal after seven centuries of English control, Plaid Cymru can take credit for helping launch the current revival in Welsh language and self-identity.

Official Monster Raving Loony Party

Who couldn't have a sneaking admiration for a political party with the catchphrase "Vote for insanity—you know it makes sense"? The party was founded by the colorful Screaming Lord Sutch, a minor rock singer who was not really a peer and was instantly recognizable in his top hat and gold lamé suit. Sutch led the party until his death in 1999, demanding to know such things as why there was only one Monopolies Commission and what was sliced bread the best invention since? Though many of the party's current proposals, such as the introduction of a 99-pence coin to save on change and legislation mandating that socks must be sold in sets of three to cover against the inevitable loss of one, might seem, well, loony, it should be remembered that ideas change in politics. The Monster Raving Loonies were the first political party in Britain to propose such seemingly loony ideas as a voting age of eighteen, passports for pets, licensing commercial radio, and all-day pub openings, all of which have come to pass (though the Loonies' 1997 election manifesto did call for revoking the broadcasting license of any radio station caught playing a Cliff Richard record, an idea yet to be taken up by any of the major parties).

BNP (British National Party)

Mentioned here only because they tend to generate a lot more media attention than their size would warrant, the BNP is the ugly face of extremist British nationalism. In the mold of Jean-Marie Le Pen's neofascists in France, the BNP advocates the expulsion of immigrants and the preservation of Britain for its "indigenous" peoples, whom they rather ridiculously describe as "people whose ancestors were the earliest settlers here after the last great Ice Age." Strictly speaking, this would lead to the exclusion of just about everyone in the British Isles today, whatever color they might be. Unfortunately, though they only poll in single digits, the BNP is a growing force. The party has some fifty town councilors elected across England, and in the 119 seats they contested in the 2005 parliamentary elections they regularly came in fourth, after the three main parties.

Northern Irish Political Parties

Living up to its reputation as a contentious place, Northern Ireland has no less than four main political parties. The Protestants and Catholics each have two, which mirror each other more than either side would care to admit. Each side has one historically moderate party and one historically militant party, which, this being Northern Ireland, does imply a connection with actual gun-toting militias.

On the Protestant side, compromise tends to be represented by the Ulster Unionist Party (UUP), while the Democratic Unionist Party (DUP) has historically been the home of those who argue for a more extremist stance and believe that papal plots and Vatican machinations lie behind most of the world's troubles. (When Pope John Paul II addressed the European parliament in 1988, the DUP's longtime leader Rev. Ian Paisley disrupted the proceedings, shouting "I denounce you, Anti-Christ! I refuse you as Christ's enemy and Antichrist with all your false doctrine.") The moderate Catholic viewpoint is voiced by the Social Democrat and Labour Party (SDLP), while Sinn Féin, Irish Gaelic for "We Ourselves," is the political wing of the IRA (Irish Republican

Army). There is actually a fifth party, the nonsectarian and centrist Alliance Party, but they have only a small representation in the Northern Irish assembly, the middle ground being a pretty desolate political place in Northern Ireland.

It is a telling comment on the ongoing tribalism of the two sides that while it was the leaders of the moderate parties on either side, the UUP's David Trimble and the SDLP's John Hume, who shared the Nobel Peace Prize in 1998 and international praise for their peacemaking efforts, they were rewarded by their own electorates with a thorough drubbing. Trimble actually lost his seat in 2005. The hardliners were rewarded for their obstructionism. The DUP and Sinn Féin became the first and second largest parties respectively in the 2007 assembly.

TWENTIETH-CENTURY
PRIME MINISTERS AND THEIR PARTIES

Name	Party	Years as Prime Minister
Gordon Brown	Labour	2007–
Tony Blair	Labour	1997–2007
John Major	Conservative	1990–97
Margaret Thatcher	Conservative	1979–90
James Callaghan	Labour	1976–79
Edward Heath	Conservative	1970–74
Harold Wilson	Labour	1974–76
		1964–70
Sir Alec Douglas-Home	Conservative	1963–64
Harold Macmillan	Conservative	1957–63
Sir Anthony Eden	Conservative	1955–57
Clement Attlee	Labour	1945–51
Sir Winston Churchill	Conservative	1940–45
		1951–55

Neville Chamberlain	Conservative	1937–40
James Ramsay MacDonald	Labour	1924, 1929–35
Stanley Baldwin	Conservative	1923–24, 1924–29, 1935–37
Andrew Bonar Law	Conservative	1922–23
David Lloyd George	Liberal	1916–22
Herbert Henry Asquith	Liberal	1908–16
Henry Campbell-Bannerman	Liberal	1905–8
Arthur James Balfour	Conservative	1902–5
Marquess of Salisbury	Conservative	1895–1902

COLORFUL CHARACTERS IN POLITICS

It can be argued that it takes a large personality to run a large city. Cases in point are the first two mayors of London to ever be elected, Ken Livingstone and Boris Johnson. Before 2000, the various boroughs that made up London each had their own governmental body without one mayor or office coordinating and overseeing the whole. The City of London has its own Lord Mayor, though that is a separate entity.

Ken Livingstone (b. 1945)

The first directly elected mayor of London, Ken Livingstone has been nicknamed "Red Ken" because of his left-wing politics. He comes from a working-class background, grew up in London, and was elected first to the Lambeth Borough Council then the GLC (Greater London Council). In 1981, he became leader of the GLC and raised the ire of Conservative prime minister Margaret Thatcher with such shenanigans as inviting leaders of Northern Ireland's Sinn Féin political party to London. Thatcher, not being one to deal in half measures, abolished the Greater London Council as well as other city councils, which were mostly Labour dominated. Livingstone had been controversial, but Thatcher turned him into a hero. He went on to become a Labour MP, then entered the race for mayor of London. After antagonizing Tony

Blair and the "New Labour" wing of the party, he was denied the Labour nomination but ran anyway and won as an independent— though he later rejoined the Labour Party. As mayor he was accused of wasteful expenditures and ruthless politics, and was given to outbursts such as comparing a Jewish reporter to a concentration camp guard. On the other hand, he is also credited with securing the 2012 Olympics for London, guiding the city through the July 7, 2005, terrorist attacks, and successfully instituting the congestion charge in central London (see page 185). He was reelected in 2004 but lost to Boris Johnson in 2008. He's known to be an avid collector of newts.

Boris Johnson (b. 1964)

Known for his rumpled suits, blond hair, bumbling manner, and verbal gaffes, Boris Johnson is the rather posh Conservative mayor of London. Born in New York to English parents (he was a dual US citizen until recently), he attended Eton and Oxford and then launched a career in journalism. He joined *The Daily Telegraph* in 1987, became a political columnist at *The Spectator* in 1994, and was named its editor in 1999. In 2001, he was elected to Parliament for the genteel Henley-on-Thames, home of the Royal Henley Regatta. Through all this, he's had a proven track record for putting his foot (or his pen) in his mouth, such as the time he had to apologize after writing in a *Telegraph* column that Papua New Guinea was known for "cannibalism and chief-killing" or the time he described Africans as having "watermelon smiles." Once he had to apologize to the entire city of Liverpool after writing that its inhabitants wallow in their "victim status." These un-PC comments and other antics made him popular with the press, always hungry for amusing fodder. When running for mayor he straightened up his act and got more serious, even giving up alcohol during the campaign.

BRITISH POLITICAL SCANDALS OF NOTE

Profumo Affair

Sex, Russian spies, and a government minister lying to Parliament—all the ingredients for a perfect political scandal. John Profumo (a dashing Conservative MP, secretary of state for war, and husband of movie star Valerie Hobson) was rumored in the media to be having an affair with a nineteen-year-old call girl he had met at Lord Astor's country house. Profumo stood up before Parliament in March 1963 and denied any hanky-panky with the beautiful young Christine Keeler. But it was a speech he was to regret. The ensuing investigation revealed not only that he'd lied to the house but also that he'd been unwittingly sharing the favors of Keeler with a Russian military attaché (read: spy). Suddenly the whole affair was elevated from a tawdry sex scandal to an issue of national security with wild speculation over what state secrets might have passed as pillow talk. By the summer, Profumo had resigned. The fallout from the affair was influential in the October resignation of Conservative prime minister Harold Macmillan and the defeat of the Conservative government the following year. The 1989 movie *Scandal* with Ian McKellen, John Hurt, and Joanne Whalley was based on the Profumo Affair.

The Cecil Parkinson and Sara Keays Saga

One of Margaret Thatcher's closest political advisers, MP and secretary of state for trade and industry Cecil Parkinson, had to resign in 1983 following revelations that he'd been having a long-term extramarital affair with his secretary Sara Keays and that she was pregnant with his child. In a scandal that kept resurfacing in the papers and courts, Parkinson opted to stay with his wife despite Keays's claims that he'd promised to marry her. Keays wrote a statement in *The Times* criticizing Parkinson's conduct, which prompted his resignation. Keays and Parkinson initially agreed to a court injunction that would keep their daughter, Flora, out of the media. Despite the injunction, Keays spoke on television in 1993 about Flora's Asperger's syndrome and disabilities resulting from an operation for a brain tumor. Keays found herself threatened with contempt of court, and a stricter injunction was put in place. Later, the court again stepped in and stopped a documentary, which Keays had approved, from showing Flora at a special school in Jerusalem. When Flora turned eighteen in 2002 the injunction was lifted and the saga continued; Keays and Flora were interviewed on television claiming that Parkinson refused to see Flora and appealing for more financial support. In the decades during which this unfolded, Parkinson was made a baron and was at two different times the Conservative Party chairman.

The David Blunkett "Who's the Daddy?" Affair

David Blunkett, a Labour MP who was named home secretary in 2001, was born blind to a working-class background. In 2004, after an email surfaced that allegedly showed his department had fast-tracked a visa application for his ex-lover's nanny, Blunkett resigned as home secretary, though remained an MP.

Left-wing Blunkett, who was divorced, had conducted a three-year affair with the married publisher of the right-wing *Spectator* magazine, Kimberley Quinn. Blunkett and Quinn broke up early in 2004, and after the split Blunkett took legal action for paternity rights and access to Quinn's two-year-old son. Quinn released allegations saying, among other things, that Blunkett had expedited her nanny's visa—the charge that resulted ultimately in his resignation as home secretary. Quinn gave birth to another son six weeks after Blunkett resigned, and DNA tests showed that Blunkett was not the father.

BRITISH POLITICAL FAQS

What's a "shadow cabinet"?
In the parliamentary system, the political party that's in power names the prime minister and the cabinet members. The second most powerful party is called "Her Majesty's Official Opposition." They, and the other opposition parties, each assemble what is called a "shadow cabinet." Since the 1920s, the Labour and Conservative parties have traded off being the party in power and the main opposition party.

The shadow cabinet, which might sound like something out of a science-fiction novel, might include a shadow chancellor of the exchequer, shadow foreign secretary, shadow home secretary, and so forth for all the positions held in the regular cabinet. Shadow ministers, whose purpose is to be a spokesman for arguments counter to those made by the party in power, develop policies according to their party's platform and beliefs. In reading the newspapers, it's common to see a shadow secretary comment on an action taken by the party in power.

What's a "backbencher"?

The front rows of the House of Commons are filled with the government's ministers and their counterparts in the opposition's shadow government. The other MPs sit in the back rows and are called "backbenchers."

Is there a constitution in the UK?

Yes and no. There is no written constitution in UK the way there is in the US. There is an "uncodified constitution," which is a group of laws passed by Parliament that defines the powers of government, as well as something called "the Royal Prerogative" and unwritten traditions. With a written constitution, there is an absolute document to refer back to that takes precedence over any laws the Congress may pass, whereas with an unwritten constitution there is no precedence, and Parliament can largely change the law as it wishes.

What was the "poll tax"?

In the beginning, homeowners in the UK paid valuation-based "rates" on their real estate to finance government, much as real estate taxes are paid in the US today. Then, in 1989, Conservative Party prime minister Margaret Thatcher thought to decouple local finances from local real estate values and introduced the community charge, whereby individuals would be taxed rather than real estate. The tax was introduced in Scotland in 1989 and the rest of the country a year later.

The poll tax, as it was quickly dubbed, was a flat tax that every adult in a locality was expected to pay, be they rich or poor, homeowner or renter, tenement dweller or mansion grandee. The unemployed and others in difficult circumstances got a reduction but not an exemption. The poll tax amount was set by local councils, so it varied from place to place, though the average was approximately £400 per person (roughly $720 at 1990 exchange rates).

The idea was that forcing everyone to pay the same amount would cause people to demand that local governments curb expenditures. That most local governments happened to be predominantly controlled by the opposition Labour Party was supposedly incidental, (though targeted subsidies permitted flagship Conservative councils to charge artificially low poll tax rates). It proved to be probably the most misconceived idea in modern British political history.

The British are a nation of grumblers, not activists, which proved to be Thatcher's undoing. To protest the poll tax you didn't actually have to do (or pay) anything—what had been just idleness yesterday suddenly became tax resistance and noble civil disobedience. Not to mention that people, being mobile, are a lot trickier to collect taxation on than stationary property. Non-payment rates of the poll tax were so high—over 30 percent in some areas—it was clear that the authorities were never going to be able to come after everyone, especially when they were preoccupied chasing down the rioters whose protests against the poll tax were ripping up city centers under the banner "Can't Pay, Won't Pay." In March 1990, a demonstration in Trafalgar Square against the tax disintegrated into the worst riots London has seen in modern times. The poll tax was the end of Maggie Thatcher's political life and was hastily replaced with the current council tax, a return to the previous real-estate-value-based system.

FACT OR FICTION?

Former prime minister Winston Churchill was known to be a teetotaler who frowned upon drinking alcohol no matter the situation.

Fiction. Winston Churchill enjoyed his alcohol and had a penchant for champagne in particular (Pol Roger was his favorite). He was famously quoted as saying, "I have taken more out of alcohol than alcohol has taken out of me." He was hardly the only prime minister with a taste for booze. William Pitt the Younger, prime minister from 1783 to 1801 and again from 1804 to 1806, reportedly drank three bottles of port a day. As the later prime minister Henry Addington, whose father had been Pitt's doctor, put it: "Mr. Pitt liked a glass of port very well, and a bottle better." The early twentieth-century Liberal prime minister Herbert Asquith's fondness for a drink was celebrated in a music-hall song with the line "Mr. Asquith says in a manner sweet and calm: Another little drink won't do us any harm." In the mid-1970s, Labour prime minister Harold Wilson was reportedly prone to knocking back a few stiff brandies before facing off against opposition leader Margaret Thatcher. Britain's political culture today, though, is less tolerant of rampant alcohol abuse, as evidenced by the recent Liberal Democrat Party leader Charles Kennedy, who was compelled to resign as party leader after admitting to a drinking problem.

Religion plays a big part in British politics. Most elected officials have to prove to their constituencies that they are faithful churchgoers.

Fiction. A politician's religion is a much more private matter in the UK than it is in the US, where politicians seem to need to prove that they are good Christians in order to win an election. Traditionally, British politics steer clear of moral issues, quite unlike the US. In Britain, when someone comments on the devoutness of a politician, they are not, as is often the case in America, insinuating that the politician in question is an extreme social conservative with views on evolution and global warming that differ significantly from the mainstream scientific consensus. They will actually just be commenting on the politician's faith.

Elections in the UK are traditionally held on Thursdays.

Fact. While the US generally has elections on Tuesdays, the UK does its voting on Thursdays.

CHAPTER 5

FOOD AND DRINK

BRITISH CUISINE AND COMFORT FOOD

Generally, when one hears the phrase "British cuisine" spoken beyond the British Isles, it is safely assumed to be the punch line to a joke—probably one that also mentions "German fashion" and "Italian road rules." Nowadays, however, the British will hotly dispute this as an outdated stereotype. And though their protests may have merit, the objective viewer can hardly be surprised at its continued currency; this is, after all, a nation whose traditional dishes, with names like spotted dick and toad-in-the-hole, sound more like slang terms for venereal disease than haute cuisine.

In truth, though, the British attitude toward food has undergone a revolution. No longer is mealtime considered a character-building trial by overcooked meat and two soggy veggies. In fact, the appreciation and enjoyment of food in the British Isles today could even be called—dare one say it?—Continental. In the past decade or two, the British have evolved to become a nation of self-styled gourmands. Supermarket shelves are piled high with organic pomegranates and grass-fed beef; dowdy old pubs have been revitalized as light and airy "gastro-pubs"; the natives are as liable to discuss soufflé recipes as the weather. The populace is now on a first-name basis with the culinary gurus of print and small screen: Delia, Gordon, Nigella, and Jamie (Smith, Ramsay, Lawson, and Oliver respectively, for the uninitiated) sweep television ratings and bestseller lists.

This is all well worth considering before cracking British food jokes in mixed company: To most Europeans, American food conjures up images of grossly obese and badly dressed people lurching from one fast-food outlet to another. Unless you're prepared to counter such not-so-entirely-inaccurate perceptions, keep the beef Wellington jokes to yourself.

SOME MATTERS OF ETIQUETTE

Passing the Port to Port

When sitting down with a group of friends to enjoy a bottle or decanter of port, it's important to remember that port is always passed to the port, which is the left for the non-nautical types out there. The host will pour a glass of port for the person sitting to his right, serve himself, and then pass the bottle to the person sitting to his left, who should pour some port and pass it along again to the left. It's bad form to fill your own glass and leave the bottle sitting in front of you, giving port-thirsty persons to your left no choice but to ask you to move it along.

Hands versus Knife and Fork

	US	UK
Asparagus	Use a knife and fork	Eat with hands
Pizza	Eat with hands	Use a knife and fork
Hamburger in a bun	Eat with hands	Use a knife and fork

FAVORITES OF THE UK

People always love junk food that reminds them of home. For a British person, this would include:

British Candy

Candy	Nearest US Equivalent	Notes
Mars bar	Milky Way	"A Mars a day helps you work, rest and play," or so ran the old ads. It is chocolate-covered nougat and caramel.
Milky Way	Three Musketeers	A Mars bar without the caramel, just chocolate and nougat.
Smarties	M&M's	Packaged in a distinctive cardboard tube. Like M&M's but bigger.
Maltesers Crunchie	Malted milk balls	But so much better. A sort of synthetic honeycomb coated with a thin layer of chocolate. Delicious.

Sherbet Fountain	Fun Dip	Powdered sugary sherbet with a stick of licorice. The wetted licorice is dipped into the sherbet and sucked off.
Flake		Bar of folded milk chocolate that crumbles in the mouth. A great national treat is a 99, which is a soft-serve vanilla ice cream cone with one of these stuck in it.
Bounty	Mounds	Coconut covered in chocolate.
Minstrels	M&M's	Oversized chocolate—inside and out—M&M's.
Curly Wurly		Braided strands of chocolate-covered caramel.
Fruit pastilles		Fruit-flavored gelatinous blobs coated in sugar. Everyone's favorites are the blackcurrant ones.
Fruit gums		Really hard and chewy fruit-flavored candies. Not for people with braces.
Polo Mints	Peppermint Life Savers	

Yorkie bar	Thick, chunky, manly milk chocolate bar. "It's not for girls!" says the packaging.

HP Sauce

Proclaiming itself "the official sauce of Great Britain," HP Sauce has been a staple of British cuisine since the early 1900s. For more than one hundred years it was manufactured in Birmingham, England. Then the US company Heinz bought HP Foods and in 2007, amid much protest, moved production of the famed sauce to the Netherlands.

HP Sauce is a combination of malted vinegar, dates, sugar, apples, tomatoes, and various spices with a tangy flavor that's a favorite on many things—from fish and chips to breakfast sausage. A picture of the Houses of Parliament (HP, get it?) on the label helps to establish it as the quintessentially British sauce (at least until the move to Holland).

The satire magazine *Private Eye*'s section on parliamentary news is called "HP Sauce."

Marmite

What is the power of this brown salty paste that it can send a British expat into deep despair when the jar is empty? Or send an unsuspecting person into fits of revulsion upon just smelling it? The strong flavor of Marmite is certainly an acquired taste and one that most Brits have been enjoying (or seriously not enjoying) since childhood.

It's made with old brewer's yeast—leftover stuff from making beer. The Marmite Food Company Limited was created in 1902 and based near the Bass Brewery in Burton upon Trent in England. After getting off to a slow start, Marmite gained popularity when it was discovered that the extracted yeast in Marmite is packed with B vitamins. Soon the salty spread was a staple in the British diet, being served to soldiers in both world wars, and in hospitals, schools, and homes around the UK.

The name comes from the French word *marmite,* which means "stockpot," though, of course, the British pronunciation (mar-mite) differs from the French (mar-meet). The key to enjoying Marmite is that it must be used sparingly. To be clear: Buttered toast must be just glazed with the stuff, otherwise it can be overpowering. Marmite on hot buttered toast or crumpets is a particular favorite; it's also used in soups and stews, on sandwiches, and to flavor crisps (potato chips).

The uninitiated might wonder what the difference is between Vegemite and Marmite. Both are vegetarian, brown, and salty. The difference is that Vegemite is made in Australia and has a slightly sweeter flavor that is, to the Marmite purist, unacceptable.

Heinz Salad Cream

It's like mayonnaise, but it isn't quite mayonnaise. Generally speaking, salad cream, a cheaper version of mayonnaise, is a condiment of choice in the north, whereas mayonnaise is found more often in the refrigerators of the south. It's a north-south thing, a class thing, and one of those things you can never truly understand. Suffice it to say, people who grew up with salad cream will prefer that while those who grew up with mayonnaise will prefer the latter. Consider the Miracle Whip versus mayonnaise debate in the US.

Branston Pickle

When you order a "cheese and pickle" sandwich, it's Branston pickle that you'll be getting, not green slices of pickled cucumber. It's a sweet and tangy condiment with an unappealing brown color—some might call it a relish. Whatever you call it, it's one of the most popular foods in Britain with a reported twenty-eight million jars of the stuff sold each year.

Branston pickle is made with carrots, rutabaga, onions, dates, cauliflower, apples, zucchini, and an assortment of other ingredients by the Crosse and Blackwell company. First made in 1922 at a factory in Branston, near Burton upon Trent, it's commonly seen in a "ploughman's lunch," a pub standard: traditionally a piece or two of bread, some cheese, a salad, and, of course, some Branston pickle.

Hob Nobs

These are cookies made with rolled oats that are available covered in milk chocolate, dark chocolate, or just plain. Made by the company McVities, they can be dunked in tea without crumbling and are a favorite in Britain.

Jaffa Cakes

Biscuit-sized, round, and made with a layer of spongy cake, orange jelly, and chocolate, Jaffa cakes are produced by a variety of brands, though McVities makes the most popular one.

Twiglets

Twig-shaped, crunchy, salty, pretzel-like snacks with a sort of burned flavor. Twiglets are made by Jacobs Bakery. They appeal to those with a taste for the salty spread Marmite.

SCOTTISH TRADITIONAL FOODS

Haggis is perhaps the best-known traditional dish from Scotland. For tourists, the desire to try haggis comes from a combination of curiosity and fear; it takes a strong stomach and a brave constitution to dig in once you know how haggis is made.

The Scottish are stereotypically thrifty, so it comes as little surprise that their famous dish is made not with the prime cuts but with the leftover bits of sheep, namely the liver, heart, and lungs. These are boiled with beef fat then chopped up and mixed with oatmeal, onions, spices, and gravy. This mixture is stuffed into a casing, which traditionally is a sheep's stomach. For those still reading and not ill, let it be known that the result is rich, savory, and actually quite tasty.

The beloved Scottish poet Robert Burns wrote the poem "Address to a Haggis," which is read at celebrations across Scotland (and wherever Scottish expats dwell) during the annual Burns Night supper held on January 25 to commemorate the poet's birthday. At these suppers, the haggis is introduced by a bagpiper, Burns's poem is read, and the sheep stomach casing is ceremoniously cut. The traditional accompaniments to haggis are mashed turnips and mashed potatoes, all washed down with copious amounts of whisky.

WELSH TRADITIONAL FOODS

When visiting Wales, you might be presented with an item of food that is black, mushy, and something common sense suggests should not go into your mouth. It may be an acquired taste, but once you come around, this **laverbread**, as it's called, is not just tasty but also supposedly packed with vitamins and minerals. It's seaweed that has been boiled and chopped up—the same type of seaweed used in Japanese cuisine. For a traditional Welsh breakfast, laverbread might be mixed with lemon juice, rolled in oatmeal, and put on toast or else fried in bacon fat and served with eggs and black pudding. Laverbread is also used to add flavor to dishes such as risotto, scrambled eggs, and fish curry.

Cawl is a traditional Welsh soup usually made with lamb (though pork, mutton, and beef are also used), leeks, turnips, parsnips, and bacon.

Bara brith is a Welsh fruit bread. It's made by soaking dried fruit in tea. The Welsh word "bara" means bread, and "brith" is speckled—so it's speckled bread.

CUISINE TERMINOLOGY

UK	US
Aubergine	Eggplant
Bangers	Sausages
Black pudding	Sausage made with pork fat and pig's blood
Brew, cuppa, cha	Tea (The British have as many words for tea as the Eskimos have for snow.)
Brown sauce	HP Brown Sauce
Bubble and squeak	Dish of reheated leftover cabbage and potatoes
Buck's fizz	Mimosa (orange juice and champagne)
Butty	Sandwich (term used mostly in the north)
Candy floss	Cotton candy
Chippy, aka chip shop	Shop selling fish and chips
Chips	French fries
Cock-a-leekie	Scottish soup made with chicken and leeks
Cornish pasty	Meat and vegetables wrapped in pastry
Courgette	Zucchini
Crisps	Potato chips
Hundreds and thousands	Sprinkles
Lump and spud	Meat and potato
Maize	Corn
Pudding	Dessert
Rasher	Slice of bacon
Rocket	Arugula
Sarney	Sandwich

Sausage roll	Oversized pig in a blanket
Scotch eggs	Eggs wrapped in deep-fried meat and breadcrumbs
Scrumpy	Cider
Shandy	Mixture of beer and ginger beer or soda
Soldiers	Rectangular pieces of toast for dipping into soft-boiled eggs
Spotted dick	Roll filled with fruity pudding
Toad-in-the-hole	Sausages cooked in batter
Trifle	Gelatinous cousin of tiramisu
Welsh rarebit (or rabbit)	Melted cheese and beer on hot toast

WHAT TO DO FOR A HOMESICK BRIT

If you see a homesick Brit curled up on a sofa, even paler than usual, humming "God Save the Queen," and sipping tea, you might consider doing a few of the following things to help:

- Pop in a *Little Britain* or a *Carry On* DVD.
- Feed him Hob Nobs, Jaffa Cakes, and Twiglets.
- Make a treacle tart (see page 160 for a recipe).
- Offer more tea.
- Prepare a slice of toast with butter and a very thin layer of Marmite, or a bowl of the cold cereal Weetabix with milk.
- If she smokes, find some Benson and Hedges (Benny Hedgehogs) or Silk Cuts.
- If it's the summertime and he is of the class that pines for Ascot, give him a Pimm's Cup (see page 160 for a recipe); if he's not, a shandy.
- Ask if he or she wants a Beano comic or a copy of the *Daily Mail*. If you get her a *Hello! Magazine,* she might protest but will probably love it.

Pimm's Cup

Whether you're at a garden party or the Wimbledon tennis matches, a Pimm's Cup is the classic, classy, and ever-refreshing summer drink of England. Pimm's No. 1 is a 50 proof gin- or vodka-based liquor. The recipe varies depending on whom you ask, but the basics are:

- *Ice*
- *1 part Pimm's No. 1*
- *2 parts lemonade soda*
- *Kirby cucumber (for garnish)*
- *Slice of lemon (for garnish)*

Fill a tall glass with ice, liquor, and soda. Stir well. Garnish with cucumber and lemon slice. Lemonade soda is difficult to find in the US. You can substitute lemonade and club soda, 7Up, or Sprite. Another option is to use ginger ale with extra lemons. Mint, apple, and strawberries can also be added.

Golden Treacle Tart

Besides being Harry Potter's favorite sweet, treacle tart is a traditional favorite all around Britain. Made with a rich pastry crust and baked in golden syrup, which is a bit like molasses but more like honey, it's a sugar bomb sure to please. Here's the recipe from the Lyle's Golden Syrup website.

- *150g (5oz) fresh wholemeal breadcrumbs*
- *225g (8oz) Lyle's Golden Syrup*
- *100g (4oz) butter*
- *225g (8oz) plain flour*
- *1 egg, separated*
- *25ml (5 tsp) water*
- *Tate & Lyle Granulated Sugar for dusting*

Lightly grease a 20cm (8 inch) loose-bottomed flan tin and preheat the oven to 180 degrees C, 350 degrees F, gas mark 4.

Mix the breadcrumbs with Lyle's Golden Syrup. In another bowl rub the butter into the flour until the mixture resembles fine breadcrumbs. Beat the egg yolk with the water and stir into the flour mixture to give a firm dough. Roll out ⅔ of the dough and use to line the flan tin. Fill the flan with the syrup mixture spreading it evenly.

Add the pastry trimmings to the remaining ⅓ of the dough and roll this out to a narrow strip, cut into thin strips and arrange them in a lattice pattern on top of the flan. Bake in the oven for 20 minutes. Carefully brush the lattice strips with lightly beaten egg white, and sprinkle with sugar. Return the flan to the oven for a further 15–20 minutes until golden brown. Serve warm with cream.

PUB ETIQUETTE

The British pub, short for "public house," brings to mind dark wood, brass beer taps, cozy armchairs, and stools gathered around small tables. Some pubs are still like that, especially out in the country, but more often than not you will find that urban pubs have been "reinvented" as theme pubs, remodeled to look like wine bars or sports bars, or rolled into the decorative scheme of some franchise. Others have been converted into "gastro-pubs," where the traditionally stodgy "pub grub" of the past—soggy pies, mushy vegetables, and wilting iceberg lettuce—has been replaced with organic field greens, poached fish, and a half-decent wine list. The decline in beer consumption, an increase in beer duty (tax), and the smoking ban have forced publicans (pub proprietors) to often regretful extremes of imagination to avoid joining the more than two dozen pubs a week that have closed in recent years.

Though recent legislation permits certain pubs to set their own hours, in general licensing laws set pub hours at 11 a.m. to 11 p.m. (sometimes later on the weekend, but rarely past 1 a.m.), and noon to 10:30 p.m. on Sundays. The logic behind extending hours was to prevent the usual rush of binge drinking before last call and the mass exodus of drunks spilling onto the streets at 11 p.m. on Friday and Saturday nights, which often degenerated into violence. It's debatable whether the later closings have helped, as any quick perusal of the daily tabloids should confirm that the UK is a binge-drinking culture no matter what time pubs close. Scotland and Northern Ireland have long had more flexible hours.

The ritual of last orders, as last call is known, is a sad moment for some, though for others it's an exciting chance to watch grown men drink four pints of beer in ten minutes—sort of like a Coney Island hot dog eating contest. The bartender rings a bell or flashes the lights at about ten minutes before closing and shouts, "Last Orders," or something similar, and the chugging begins. It doesn't end until the bartender shouts, "Time, please," at which point everyone is herded out into the night.

THE BRITISH AND THEIR BEER

It's a toss-up to say whether the British love their tea or their beer more. The answer would probably depend on whom you ask and what time of day it is. Tea merchants and brewers would probably argue that the Brits are losing their love for both: In 1955, the UK and Ireland accounted for a third of the world's tea consumption; today it's about 5 percent; beer sales have fallen to their lowest level since 1975. None of this, however, affects the sentimental place beer holds in British culture and its near ubiquitous availability. Americans visiting the UK might be surprised that the British pint is twenty fluid ounces, in contrast to the American sixteen, but then Americans may also be surprised by how generally boozy British culture is.

Broadly speaking, when the British say "beer," they mean ale. Ale is the general term for a type of nut-brown beer that has comparatively fruity or yeasty flavors.

"Bitter" is the most commonly found ale in England and is amber or golden in color, low in carbonation, and served at room temperature or slightly chilled. India pale ale (IPA) is a type of bitter, as are pale ale, special, and extra special bitter (ESB). What you'll find on tap is largely dependent on where you are in the country and who owns the pub you're in, but famous bitters include Bass, Tetley's, John Smith's, and Boddingtons.

In Scotland, ale was traditionally categorized by the tax paid on a barrel, which was determined by the strength of the beer. Today, you'll find 60/-, 70/-, 80/-, and even 90/- beer—the higher the number, the darker and stronger the beer. The "/-" symbol refers to the old monetary unit of a shilling, so you order "a pint of eighty shilling," "a pint of eighty," or even, for 80 shilling beer, "a pint of heavy." Ninety shilling is very strong stuff with an alcohol content north of 6 percent—be warned. Caledonian, Belhaven, and McEwan's are all popular and palatable brands.

There are other dark beers available, such as porter and stout. Dark and malty, porter was very popular a century ago, but is now seen only occasionally. Stouts, such as Guinness, Murphy's, and Beamish, are actually an offshoot of porter and were originally called stout porters. Most every pub will offer at least Guinness. You will also usually find a cider on tap. British cider, it should be pointed out, is alcoholic, with the same alcohol content as beer, and perhaps even a little more.

When Americans say "beer," they tend to mean what in England is called "lager." Lager is fermented at cooler temperatures than ale and for longer periods of time, giving it a lighter, more subtle flavor. Light, clear, and cold, this has become is the most popular type of beer in the UK. You might hear someone brag "I drank eight pints of lager last night," as it's a beer easily consumed in volume, and, to make a broad generalization, the type of people who boast about their alcohol consumption tend to be lager drinkers. Drunken youth are commonly referred to as "lager louts," and old-timers will mutter about a correlation between the rise of hooliganism among the youth and the ascendancy of lager over ale. The youth of today get their kicks as well from "alcopops," sugary, fruit-flavored alcoholic beverages.

On a cultural aside, Stella Artois in the US positions itself as a relatively upscale foreign beer. In the UK, however, it is considered so lowbrow that it has been dubbed with the nickname "wife beater" as in, "I had three pints of wife beater then left the pub." The manufacturer has responded by rebranding it as just Artois.

PUB FAQS

What's the drinking age in the UK?
You must be eighteen years old to legally buy alcohol in the UK. Given the trend of underage and binge drinking, there have been calls to raise the legal drinking age to twenty-one.

What's the difference between a "tied house" and a "free house"?
A tied house is owned by a particular brewing company and serves almost entirely beers produced by that brewery. A free house is independently owned and can serve whatever beers the proprietor wishes.

What's a "pub quiz"?
The format can vary, but generally speaking, pub quizzes happen at pubs (or other venues) on weekday evenings when they're trying to get more people in to drink. Pieces of blank paper may be passed around and teams formed. The team decides on a name, writes it at the top of the paper, and then records the answers to questions of varying degrees of difficulty. Usually there's a small fee to enter and prize money for the winning team.

What's the difference between a "saloon bar" and a "public bar"?
In older pubs you might well find two entrances, one with a sign saying "Saloon Bar" and the other door marked "Public Bar." It used to be that the saloon bar was more comfortable and a bit more expensive than the public bar, though that distinction no longer exists.

BASIC POINTS OF ETIQUETTE IN A PUB

- Order your drinks at the bar. With rare exceptions there is no wait service for drinks in pubs, though there may be for food.
- Order stouts, such as Guinness, first as they take time to pour and settle properly.
- Don't call anyone "mate" unless you've served on a boat with him.
- Don't leave a tip when ordering drinks. The publican is your equal, so you can offer to buy him a drink if you feel compelled to show your gratitude. If you sit at a table, order food, and have it brought to you, then tip as if at a restaurant (about 10 percent).
- Pay for your drinks when you order them. Unless you are ordering food, the publican is unlikely to let you run a tab.
- Be prepared to pay cash. Though credit cards are accepted at more and more pubs today, never assume you can pay with one.

FACT OR FICTION?

The leek is a national emblem of Wales.

Fact. Don't be surprised to see Welsh people sporting a leek on their hat or their lapels. This is most likely to happen on March 1, Saint David's Day, which honors the patron saint of Wales.

One theory on the origin of this is that during a seventh-century battle with the Saxons held in a field of leeks, the Welsh were thought to have worn the vegetable in their hats to distinguish themselves from the enemy—a tactic that helped them win. Some £1 coins, those honoring Wales, have leeks on the reverse side.

After drinking ten pints of lager, it would be typical to go out for Indian food.

Fact. Late-night pizza in the US equals tikka masala, some curry dish, or a kebab in the UK.

A sure way to make friends in a pub is to complain about the beer.

Fiction. As an American, a sure way to insult your company is to complain about the beer served in pubs. Brits generally don't think Americans have a leg to stand on, coming from the land of Pabst Blue Ribbon and Bud Lite.

It is customary to leave a 10 percent tip at restaurants.

Fact. If the service has been good, a 10 percent tip for your waiter is appropriate. Check bills to ensure that a service charge hasn't already been included, in which case there's no need to leave a tip.

CHAPTER 6

LANGUAGE

WEIRD PRONUNCIATIONS

Everything is not as it appears. The pronunciation of certain names is impossible to guess by simply reading them. Attempts to phonetically unravel names including "Althorp," "Thames," "Beauchamps," and "Pall Mall" will only lead to ridicule.

PRONUNCIATION GUIDE

Althorp. The ancestral home of the Spencer family, as in Princess Diana, is actually pronounced "all-trupp." Remarkably, this peculiar switching of the "o" and the "r" predates the death of Diana and the need for secret pronunciations to differentiate the tourist from the insider.

Beauchamps. Another example of the terrible things the British have done to a perfectly good French word, Beauchamps is pronounced "beecham."

Berkeley. Berkeley Square is pronounced "barclay square." Berkshire, a county outside of London, is pronounced "bark-sheer."

Cockburn. Best not to sound this one out; it's "co-bun."

Derby. If you're off to the derby, remember it's pronounced the "darby."

Hertfordshire. The county just outside of London is pronounced "hart-fordsheer."

Leicester Square. The tourist hub of London is pronounced "lester square."

Magdalen. Magdalen College at Oxford is pronounced "maudelen."

Pall Mall. The avenue stretching from St. James's to Trafalgar Square takes its peculiar name from an even more peculiar seventeenth-century sport, a sort of precursor to croquet, which used to be played on the site. It is pronounced "pal mal," or more old-fashionedly, "pel mel."

Saint John. This is a surname that is pronounced "sin jun."

Thames. The river running through London is the "tems."

COCKNEY

According to London tradition, to be a true Cockney one must have been born within listening distance of the bells of St. Mary-Le-Bow

Church in the City of London. With the wailing sirens, screeching buses, and pounding jackhammers of the modern era, that pretty much limits you to about a one-block circumference around the church, an area that today is composed of office blocks and is quite devoid of a maternity unit. However, in past centuries this would have encompassed much of the traditionally working-class East End of London. That these boundaries need to have been so firmly stated as far back as the seventeenth century is indicative of just how long the sons of the middle-classes have been aspiring to ghetto-chic.

During the Victorian era, the traditional shipyards and light industry of the East End became obsolete, and the area became a watchword for poverty and vice, inhabited by such alluring characters, both real and imagined, as Jack the Ripper and the Dickens characters Fagin and the Artful Dodger. Even that caricature of the inscrutably evil Oriental, Dr. Fu-Manchu, was depicted in his original literary incarnation as a dark shadow flitting between the warehouses and opium dens of this vast slum.

An upper-class person who assumes a Cockney accent or manner to gain street cred is called a "mockney."

RHYMING SLANG

One of the enduring legacies of the Cockneys is their peculiar form of rhyming slang. There are numerous theories about its origin; perhaps it was developed to provide a method of communication impenetrable to outsiders, and in particular the forces of law and order. Whatever its roots might be, it's rather fun. Essentially, this form of slang replaces a regular word with a phrase rhyming with it. Thus, the telephone becomes the "dog and bone." The tricky thing is that the phrase is often abbreviated to the non-rhyming part. So, an American visitor might be called a "septic," not in allusion to their cleanliness but simply because "septic tank" rhymes with "Yank."

Like any living language, Cockney rhyming slang is a constantly evolving argot. Thus, the popular English television host Emma Freud has had to endure her name becoming a synonym for hemorrhoid—an "Emma"—and the DJ Pete Tong's name has entered the vernacular as a substitute for the word "wrong"—"Pete." If you didn't get to the Fatboy Slim (gym), maybe it's because you were off having a Melvyn Bragg (shag).

What You Hear	What It Means	What It Comes From
"have a butcher's"	have a look	butcher's hook
"telling porkies"	telling lies	pork pies
"hit him in the boat"	hit him in the face	boat race
"he's got big plates"	he's got big feet	plates of meat
"on the dog"	on the phone	dog and bone
"my trouble's not well"	my wife's not well	trouble and strife
"my old china"	my old mate	china plate
"pint at the nuclear"	pint at the pub	nuclear sub
"smashed his Chevy"	smashed his face	Chevy Chase
"nice bacons"	nice legs	bacon and eggs
"have a Britney"	have a beer	Britney Spears
"I'm off for an Eartha"	I'm off for a shit	Eartha Kitt
"he's a bit of a ginger"	he's a bit of a queer	ginger beer
"I don't have a Scooby"	I don't have a clue	Scooby-Doo
"I've got my saucepans"	I've got my kids	saucepan lids

LOST IN TRANSLATION— SEPARATED BY A COMMON TONGUE

Certain words and phrases have meanings that are more or less naughty, suggestive, offensive, or giggle worthy when uttered in the UK. While the huge amount of movies and television programs imported from the US have made the average British person aware of many Americanisms, it's still a good idea to keep the following in mind.

Randy

Should you introduce yourself by saying "Hi! I'm Randy," don't take the resulting snickers personally. You've just informed your new acquaintance of your state of sexual arousal.

Roger

To "roger" is to have one's way with someone—in a coarse, not very romantic sort of fashion. Just for fun, emphatically tell a British person that "Roger Rabbit" is your favorite cartoon character. Try to say "Roger Rabbit" a few times in a row and see what the reaction is.

Spunk

If you describe a vivacious person as having lots of spunk, be warned that in British parlance you've commented on the volume of their semen. It's much worse to call a girl, rather than a boy, spunky.

A challenge! Try saying, "Have you met my friend Randy? He's so spunky, you'll love him," and see what happens.

Khaki Pants

When discussing your outfits, keep in mind that telling people you plan to wear "khaki pants" to a party may sound like you'll be arriving in poopy underwear.

The trouble begins with the fact that in Britain, "pants" means "underwear" and "trousers" are what you wear over your pants. While the British do wear "khaki trousers," their pronunciation of "khaki" has a rounder, fuller bodied "a" (khah-ki) than the same word said with an American accent (ka-ki). The American pronunciation of "khaki" tends to sound like the British slang word "cacky," meaning dirty or poopy.

Fanny

"Fanny" means "pussy." Some travelers like to keep their valuable possessions in a small pouch that is worn around the waist and called a "fanny pack." In Britain, "fanny pack" translates as "vagina pack," which is really not something you want to discuss in company. "Bum bag" would be a more appropriate term to use.

The Peace Sign versus Flipping Someone Off

In the US, we give people the finger to tell them to f-off. In the UK, they do it differently, using a fist, with the palm facing themselves and the index and middle fingers pointed up to create a V. The common, though probably incorrect, origin given for this sign is that it was invented at the Battle of Agincourt in 1415 by the English and Welsh archers, who used it to taunt the French and remind them of the superiority of the British longbow. This British hand expression is easily confused with the universal V-fingered hand sign for peace or victory, except that in Britain peace (or victory) requires the palm be facing out. Winston Churchill made the "V" for victory sign famous—he was not telling his countrymen to f-off.

To avoid unintended offense in the UK, it's a good idea to think twice before flashing the old victory sign with your palm facing toward you.

THE ODDNESS OF BRITISH NICKNAMES

The British have a knack for assigning nicknames. When reading the newspaper, you shouldn't have to ask who Keef or Chaz is. Here are a few commonly seen nicknames.

> Macca = Paul McCartney
> Mucca = Heather Mills McCartney
> Jacko, aka Wacko Jacko = Michael Jackson
> Chaz = Prince Charles
> Gazza = footballer Paul Gascoigne
> Keef = Keith Richards
> Madge = Madonna

SWEAR WORDS: HOW OFFENSIVE ARE THEY?

When swear words aren't your own, it's difficult to know just how offensive they are. If someone calls you a "tosser," does he want to be your friend? How shocking is it to say someone is a "wanker"? It is best, of course, to stick with your own swear words, but to give you some guidelines on interpreting the level of vulgarity and offensiveness in swear words of the UK, we offer the following rating system.

4. Kicked out of the pub / Wouldn't dare say in front of your mum
3. Out with the lads / Slapped by your mum
2. Chatting with the boss / Your mum would scold you
1. Tea with the vicar / Your mum would use it

Blimey
"Blimey," part of the less frequently heard phrase "cor blimey," is derived from the phrase "God blind me." It is a mild swear word that expresses surprise.

Example: "Blimey, it's late."
Rating: 1–2

Bloody
"Bloody" is used for emphasis. Not terribly rude, it's on par with "damn." It is thought to refer to the blood of Christ, but those whose livelihood lies in the study of such things disagree on the etymology.

Examples: "Bloody hell!" (How surprising!)
"Bloody great time" (What fun!)
Rating: 2

Blooming

A modifier used for emphasis.

> Example: "It's blooming cold outside!"
> Rating: 1

Bollocks

Balls. Means "nonsense" or, as an exclamation, shows frustration or anger. In 1977, the Sex Pistols released their album *Never Mind the Bollocks, Here's the Sex Pistols,* which caused controversy due to the word "bollocks" in the title.

> Example: "What a load of bollocks!"
> Example: "Bollocks! I'm locked out of my car."
> Rating: 2.5

Bugger

"Bugger" means "anal sex," and the word can be used to express annoyance or frustration. Also you can call someone a "bugger" in a pitying sense, as in "that poor bugger." "Bugger-all" means "nothing," as in "I've got bugger-all to do tonight."

> Example: "Bugger off."
> Rating: 3

Slag

A "slag" is a prostitute or a floozy, perhaps of the elder sort. A loose woman might also be called a "slapper" or a "tart."

> Example: "Look at that slag all tarted up for the evening."
> Rating: 3

Tosser

A slightly milder form of "wanker" (see below), a "tosser" is one who masturbates or is just a general jerk. It's used to describe a male; you wouldn't call a female a tosser. It's a pretty strong word to say to someone's face.

Example: "That tosser just cut the queue [line]."

Rating: 2.5

Wanker

"Wank" is synonymous with "masturbation." The term is used pretty exclusively to describe a male and carries the same intimations as "bastard." Call the bartender this and you will be turfed out of the pub.

Example: "What a wanker that copper was to give me a ticket."

Rating: 4

DICK WORDS OF THE UK

Willy = Dick

Knob or knobber = Dick

Hampton = Dick

John Thomas = Dick

Bishop = Dick

Dick = Dick

THE WELSH LANGUAGE

Though Welsh is a language of great antiquity, one wonders if its miserly distribution of vowels and limited range of consonants might

not be the result of the French and Italians taking overgenerous serv-
ings of *a*'s, *e*'s, *i*'s, *s*'s, and *t*'s as the miracle of human language fanned
west to the farthest points of Europe. We leave such musings to professional linguists. Should, however, there ever be a Welsh language
version of the game show *Wheel of Fortune,* it will probably be the letters *l, w,* and *y* that the contestants will have to purchase.

Today it stands as a great point of national identity for Welsh people.
It was, they point out, the earliest British language. Welsh fell on difficult times, though; by the sixteenth century English was the official
language of Wales, and in the twentieth century a flood of English
workers into Wales outnumbered native Welsh speakers. But there has
been a recent resurgence of sorts. Today you'll hear Welsh spoken in
the countryside of Wales and, curiously enough, in Argentina.

In the 1860s, Welsh settlers looking for independence and improved
national identity colonized a section of Patagonia at the southern tip of
Argentina. To this day, particularly in the town of Gaiman, Welsh tea-
houses abound and the language is blossoming as the Welsh traditions
take on their own unique Argentinean rhythm. The writer Bruce
Chatwin wrote extensively about the Welsh colonies in Argentina in his
book *In Patagonia.*

FIVE WELSH WORDS (AND HOW TO PRONOUNCE THEM)

Welsh Word	Means	Rough Pronunciation
mynydd	mountain	"munnith"
ysbyty	hospital	"uss-buttie"
cwm	valley	"koom"
eglwys	church	"egg-louis"
hwyl	good-bye	"who-il"

PREVALENT BRITISH NAMES RARELY HEARD IN THE US

Boys

Alistair (Scottish)

Angus (Scottish)

Ashley

Dale

Darren

Gavin

Graham

Hamish (Scottish)

Hillary

Leslie

Lionel

Martin

Nigel

Reg (short for Reginald)

Rhys (Welsh)

Rupert

Girls

Lettice

Sonya

Honor

Imogen

Philippa

Siobhan (Irish)

FACT OR FICTION?

There is little, if any, prejudice about regional accents in Britain.

Fiction. There are very real social and professional prejudices about regional accents in Britain. Frequently these mirror local rivalries, such as that between Manchester and Liverpool, or even the north and the south divide. On a professional level, the implications of this prejudice, however unconscious it might be, can be far reaching. In a much-reported survey of business executives a few years ago, 64 percent considered people with a Liverpudlian accent to be "generally unsuccessful," 77 percent reported those with a Home Counties (the region around London) accent to be "generally successful," and only 29 percent thought those with a Welsh or West Country accent to be "hardworking." Of course, this being Britain, people reflect their prejudices on themselves as much as on those around them: In 2008, *The Daily Telegraph* reported a poll showing nearly eight out of ten residents of Birmingham, Britain's second largest city, wished they had a different accent.

"Estuary English" is a slang term for the scientific lingo biologists use.

Fiction. It's the English accent spoken in southeast England around the River Thames and its estuaries, that is, around London, Essex, and Kent. The term was coined in 1984 by linguist David Rosewarne for this dialect, which mixes middle-class and working-class accents. Adopting this accent, in theory, helps make an upper-class person seem more approachable and a lower-class person better educated. Former prime minister Tony Blair was said to slip into estuary English depending on his audience. Many television hosts speak estuary English.

If someone shouts "oi" at you, he's trying to get your attention.

Fact. "Oi" is a commonly used slang term. It's like shouting "Hey you!"

CHAPTER 7

THE QUOTIDIAN

TRANSPORTATION

Americans in particular will be struck by the frequency with which conversation in the British Isles will turn to the dire state of the nation's public transportation system. In the States, discussions of the national infrastructure don't happen much outside of think tanks and university symposiums; in contrast, if you arrive at a cocktail party in the UK where you don't know many of the other guests, you can effectively break the ice by announcing your apologies for being late—even if you're quite punctual—and blame it on the bus, underground, or train.

A passing familiarity with the transportation system will convince your hosts that this is not mere idle chatter. In the US, which has never made any serious efforts toward a national public transportation system, expectations are low, but Europe and the British Isles have made real efforts and investments in their mass transit systems in the past few decades.

Furthermore, as a foreigner, your input will be authentically welcomed. Comparisons with your own native transportation system will be appreciated—the failings of the UK's travel infrastructure in comparison with that of other countries being a particularly popular angle for this line of conversation. After some time spent discussing this subject, you might be forgiven the suspicion that the British almost take a sneaking pride in the dilapidated state of their trains and buses, secretly relishing yet another difference between themselves and the Germans, Swiss, and other "Continentals." Of course, every public transport system is less than the sum of its parts, but in Britain, what are these pieces?

BUSES

In the popular imagination, Britain is the land of the red double-decker bus, with a cheery conductor welcoming all aboard the open-rear platform and allowing passengers to hop on and off at their convenience. Unfortunately, not many buses are red nowadays. Instead, they sport the colors and designs of myriad privatized carriers and regional transportation services, all hoping that a splash of distinctive paint will show how innovative their ideas are for improving the transportation system. Needless to say, these fresh ideas for improvement have included laying off the bus conductors of old and dumping their duties on the already overburdened drivers. The famous old Routemaster double-deckers have been retired and the open platform entrance done away with, legal counsel in all likelihood having decided such passenger freedom of egress could only be hazardous.

A minor cultural reference point on the subject of buses: Just before the climax of the Beatles' song "A Day in the Life," the epic conclusion of their *Sgt. Pepper's Lonely Hearts Club Band* LP, Paul McCartney sings that he "Made the bus in seconds flat [no doubt, thanks to the accessibility of the old Routemasters] / Found my way upstairs and had a smoke." While we cannot comment on the legality of what Sir Paul might have been smoking (and the BBC found it suspicious enough to ban the song from radio airplay on its 1967 release), it should be noted that he was law abiding enough to head "upstairs," the upper level being the designated smoking section on the old double-deckers.

THE UNDERGROUND

Other cities might have metros, loops, T's, and subways, but only London has the Tube. Londoners are immensely proud of the London Underground, as it is officially called, so don't be fooled by the frequency with which they complain about it. It is common to hear people moan about whatever particular line they live on (that is, at least, until someone who lives on the Northern Line approaches, at which point the argument must be ceded).

The London Underground's system map is justifiably iconic. It makes no concessions to aboveground scale but is unrivalled in its clarity and ease of use. It will come as no surprise to learn that the original was created by an electric engineer named Harry Beck, who modeled it on one of the circuit diagrams of his profession. Nearly every London Underground platform has a monitor displaying the time remaining until the next train arrives, a feature that plenty of other cities would do well to imitate.

The Tube is the oldest and the longest underground system in the world, with more than 250 miles of tracks. Some of the lines, like the District, run near the surface and aboveground. Others, like the Jubilee and Central, can alarm the novice with the sheer number of escalators required to reach their platforms.

The most striking feature of this mechanical marvel is the huge expense required to enjoy it—somewhere north of five dollars for a single one-way ticket. Or perhaps it is premature to call this the most striking feature: Before discovering how expensive it is, any visitor will be amazed by the queues that form at the ticket booths and baffled by the complexity of ticketing options. Which of the "zones" does their destination lie in? Are they traveling "off-peak"? What sort of ticket are they after: an Oyster or a Travelcard? Most will give up and buy simple one-way tickets. It goes almost without saying that these are the most expensive.

(In general, the one- or three-day Travelcard is the most convenient for a visitor. If you're not traveling during morning rush hour, the off-peak version is almost half the cost but precludes travel before 9:30 a.m. A Travelcard must be valid for all the zones you plan to travel through. Three-day Travelcards can be bought for zones 1–2 or zones 1–6, whereas one-day Travelcards can be bought for zones 1–2, 1–3, 1–4, 1–5, 1–6, and 1–9. The more zones a card is good for the more expensive it will be.)

CAR

Besides the major difference of driving on the left versus the right side of the road, there are a couple of things to note about driving in the UK.

Manual shift cars are more common, so if you're renting a car don't assume you'll get an automatic. It's best to specifically ask for an automatic, especially since, if you're not used to it, shifting gears with your left hand can be an added challenge.

While right on red is generally legal in the US, in the UK, at this point, *left* on red is not.

Car Travel Terminology

A-road. A main road, though not a motorway, that runs between major cities and towns. A-roads are numbered; for example, the road between London and Edinburgh is the A1.

Belisha beacon. A striped pole with a globe on top at a pedestrian crossing.

Bonnet. Car hood.

Boot. Car trunk.

Box junction. A yellow square, with crisscrossed lines inside it, painted on the road at an intersection. There should be only one vehicle inside the box at a time.

B-road. A minor road that typically connects two A-roads.

Dual carriageway. A road with a median and typically two lanes of traffic going each direction.

Give Way. Yield.

L-driver. Someone learning to drive. This person, who must be at least seventeen years old, holds a "provisional license," similar to a learner's permit in the US. You'll see white stickers with the letter *L* on the back of learners' cars.

MOT. Ministry of Transport test. It's like an inspection in the US; a car must pass the MOT each year after the car is three years old.

Motorway. A major multilane road for fast-moving traffic, similar to a highway in the US. The M1 is the motorway between London and the north of England; the M4 connects London and South Wales; the M11 connects London to Cambridge; the M25, a very busy road, circles around London; and the M60 circles around Manchester.

Registration number. The number on the license plates of a car—though, instead of license plates, they are called "number plates."

Sleeping policeman. A low bump running across a road to keep cars from going too fast. The same as a "speed bump" in the US.

Zebra crossing. A pedestrian crossing with black-and-white stripes.

TRAIN

The railroad system in the UK was privatized in the 1990s, which might at first sound like a good development. You'll be hard-pressed, though, to find someone with something positive to say about it. For starters, the fares are growing increasingly expensive, and different companies run different train lines, so the schedules are not necessarily in sync and can be quite confusing. Another complaint is that while one company operates the train, another entity is in charge of the track or the platform, which leads to complications and endless passing of blame. So, not surprisingly, there are calls for the system to be renationalized.

TRAINSPOTTING

Some people watch birds, others collect coins, but only the British get really excited by trains. Who else but the British would stand at the end of an empty railway platform, out in the wind and rain, jotting down the unique number and type of every locomotive that passes by? Perhaps it is a mark of that famed Anglo-Saxon eccentricity, though even in Britain trainspotters are held up as geeks par excellence, badly dressed and bereft of social skills.

Anyone who displays an overly obsessive devotion to something considered utterly boring by the majority of observers might be ribbed for being a "trainspotter" and branded an "anorak," in tribute to the type of unstylish waterproof jacket preferred by the trainspotting fraternity.

THE KNOWLEDGE

In a city such as New York, it's not uncommon to get into a taxi and find yourself giving directions to the driver. After all, there's no guarantee that your driver will speak English, have showered in the past week, or be at all sane.

In London, this is a very different story. When you step into one of its iconic black taxis you can be assured that your driver will be fluent in "the Knowledge," which is a complete familiarity with all destinations in a six-mile radius of Charing Cross at the center of London. To put this into perspective, it takes around three years to memorize the twenty-five thousand or so possible routes. There are "Knowledge Schools" that help aspiring taxi drivers pass the extensive tests to become a full-fledged taxi driver. The volume and complexity of information that a London taxi driver must learn is so vast that studies have shown the brains of London taxi drivers actually expand in the regions that deal with navigation. Students of the Knowledge can be seen around London on motorbikes with a clipboard.

Though London taxis are expensive, they also offer a first-rate experience. For a discounted ride through the city, there are car services and minibuses that you can telephone to come pick you up—these drivers will not have the Knowledge.

THE CONGESTION CHARGE

Though controversial, the congestion charge in London has cut down on the number of cars driving into the center of the city. Former Labour Party mayor of London Ken Livingstone implemented the congestion charge in 2003. Basically, to drive a private car into central London, within the congestion zone, you have to pay £8 for the day, though if you live in the zone you get a 90 percent discount. You can also buy monthly or annual passes for a discount. Cameras throughout the zone enforce the law. Taxis, disabled drivers, most two-wheeled vehicles, emergency services vehicles, and cars that use alternative energy are exempt.

The money from the charge is put toward London's transport infrastructure, such as increasing the number of buses. Besides cutting down on the amount of traffic, the congestion charge is meant to cut down on the pollution in central London. While the Labour Party supported the congestion charge, the Conservatives opposed it, and London's new Conservative mayor Boris Johnson has said he won't expand the congestion zone and will repeal its latest expansion. Johnson also abandoned Ken Livingstone's plan to introduce a daily charge of £25 for gas-guzzling 4x4s, or "Chelsea tractors," as they are sometimes known.

THINGS THE BRITISH LIKE TO GRUMBLE ABOUT

The failure of the national football team

The privatized railroad system

Mass transit in general

The French

Mud at Glastonbury (see page 102)

The weather

New Russian wealth

Immigration policies

The National Health Service

The euro

The nation's inability to cope with snow

Australians in London on gap year (see page 203)

The manager of the national football team

HOLIDAYS

Every year in England, there are six bank holidays and two public holidays. Many nonbanking businesses are also closed on bank holidays. It doesn't go unnoticed in the UK that European countries generally have more holidays than they do, which leads to ongoing proposals to add new holidays to the existing list.

CURRENT UK HOLIDAYS

New Year's Day
Good Friday (the Friday before Easter)
Easter Monday (the Monday after Easter)
Early May (the first Monday in May)
Spring bank holiday (the last Monday in May)
Summer bank holiday (the last Monday in August)
Christmas Day
Boxing Day (December 26)

Scotland also has holidays on January 2 (they need two days to recover from Hogmanay, the Scottish New Year's Eve) and Saint Andrew's Day (November 30 or, if that falls on a weekend, the following Monday). Easter Monday is not officially a holiday in Scotland, though many businesses close; the summer bank holiday is taken on the first, instead of the last, Monday in August.

Northern Ireland also has a holiday on Saint Patrick's Day (March 17) and another on the anniversary of the Battle of the Boyne (July 12).

Wales has the same holidays as England.

BRITS ON HOLIDAY

The British tend to congregate in places they used to own, such as former colonies India, Australia, New Zealand, Seychelles, Hong Kong, and Barbados. Some favorite getaway spots, divided into high-end and lower-end categories:

Top British Vacations Spots—Port Edition

- Val d'Isère, France
- Klosters, Switzerland
- Tuscany, Italy
- Barbados

- Maldives
- Seychelles
- Scottish Highlands
- Cornwall, England

Top British Vacation Spots—Lager Edition

- Benidorm, Spain
- Blackpool, England
- Butlin's Holiday Camps, England
- Ayia Napa, Fuengirola, and other Canary Islands
- Pattaya, Thailand
- Magaluf in Majorca, Spain
- Laganas in Zante, Greece
- Kavos in Corfu, Greece

Places the British Wish They Still Colonized

- Miami, Florida, in the US
- Seychelles
- Sri Lanka
- Australia (minus the Australians)
- Canada

Nations They Formerly Ruled and Can Live Without

- Zimbabwe
- South Africa

FESTIVALS

May Day, which is on May 1, celebrates the arrival of spring. The traditional festivities include setting up a Maypole, dancing around it, and crowning a May king and queen. In the nineteenth century, May 1 was designated a workers' holiday by socialist groups, and in some countries, including the UK, it's celebrated like Labor Day in the US.

Guy Fawkes Day, also called **Bonfire Night,** is celebrated on November 5 and includes fireworks, bonfires, and burning effigies of Guy Fawkes, a Catholic convert and conspirator in the foiled Gunpowder Plot of 1605 to blow up the Parliament as payback for oppression of Catholics in England. As part of the tradition, children go around asking for "a penny for the Guy," raising money, theoretically, for the bonfire. The conspirators of the Gunpowder Plot were discovered and gruesomely executed.

Remembrance Day, also known as **Poppy Day,** commemorates the sacrifices made by those who fought in wars for the country—similar to Veterans Day in the US. It's celebrated on November 11, the day that World War I officially ended in 1918. At 11 a.m. on that day the country observes two minutes of silence. People traditionally wear artificial poppy flowers in their lapels, sold to raise money for war veterans.

Burns Night, honoring the Scottish poet and national icon Robert Burns, is held each January 25 on what was believed to be his birthday. A traditional Burns supper includes potatoes, turnips, and haggis (see page 156) which is ceremoniously presented while bagpipes play and Burns's poem "Address to a Haggis" is read.

BUSINESS

In the past, the American business traveler to Britain would have found a very different culture from that back home, especially in the City of London, the financial center of the UK. Lunches were long and boozy, the banter was openly sexist, and hiring was more about social connections than qualifications. Nowadays that has all changed, and business practices in Manchester are pretty much what they are in Cleveland; in London, the pace is not much different from that of New York.

The main business area has expanded well beyond the City of London into the West End and out to Canary Wharf in the east. After London, Edinburgh is the most dynamic business center in Britain. The Scottish capital's strong banking, insurance, and service industries give it the most robust economy, per capita, in the UK.

Business Casual

"Business casual" has caught on in Britain, if not quite as widely as in the US. Like anywhere, the dress code really depends on the industry and the particular corporate culture of a company. In banking and financial services in Central London, as in other cities, men may still wear suits every day. The safest bet, if you're going into a new office, is to ask in advance or to err on the side of formality.

MOGULS OF THE UK

Mogul	Where's the Fortune From?
Sir Richard Branson	The Virgin Group (records, air travel, trains, and so on)
Sir Alan Sugar	Amstrad (an electronics company)
Duke of Westminster	UK's biggest landowner
Roman Abramovich	Oil (he's Russian, though he owns Chelsea football club)
Lakshmi Mittal	Steel (he's Indian but lives in London)

EXCHANGES

The London Stock Exchange (LSE) traces its roots back to 1698 when a certain John Castaing began to issue lists of stock and commodity prices from his "office" at a coffeehouse in London called Jonathan's. So attached to the coffeehouse lifestyle were early London stockbrokers that they briefly named their stock exchange New Jonathan's. In 2001, the two hundredth anniversary of the LSE's existence as a formal, regulated organization, it went public, floating itself as the London Stock Exchange PLC. ("PLC" stands for "public limited company" and indicates a limited liability corporation permitted to issue stock; it is similar to the US "Corp." after a company name.)

There are other specialized exchanges, such as the Alternative Investment Market (AIM), PLUS Markets, and the London International Financial Futures and Options Exchange (LIFFE, pronounced "life").

INDEXES

Just as everyone follows the Dow Jones Industrial Average in the US, in the UK the lead market indicator is the FTSE 100 (pronounced "footsie"). The initials stand for *Financial Times* Stock Exchange. The FTSE 100 tracks the one hundred most highly capitalized blue-chip firms in the UK and is perhaps more similar to the S&P 500 than the Dow Jones, whose index is a calculated figure derived from the price of thirty hand-picked stocks.

The FTSE 250 follows the mid-cap market, like the American S&P MidCap 400. FTSE's All-Share index is a combination of the FTSE 100, FTSE 250, and FTSE Small Cap indexes, which, combined, represent approximately 98 percent of the UK market capitalization. There are other indexes farther afield, such as the FTSEurofirst 300, which reflects the shares of the 300 largest companies, by market capitalization, in the FTSE Developed Europe index. The FTSE Group is an independent company jointly owned by the *Financial Times* newspaper and the London Stock Exchange.

REGULATORY AND OVERSIGHT BODIES

Following is a listing of some of the main regulatory bodies in the UK.

The Advertising Standards Authority (ASA) is the advertising industry's self-regulatory body.

The Environment Agency is the government body that serves to protect the environment and enforce environmental laws.

The Financial Services Authority (FSA) regulates all financial service providers in the UK. Although it is technically a nongovernmental office, the FSA is accountable to the Treasury and has enforcement powers.

The Office of Fair Trading (OFT) is the government agency tasked with promoting and protecting consumer interests.

Utility Regulators

In the UK, the names of regulatory bodies overseeing privatized industries tend to start with the letters OF.

The Office of Communications (OFCOM) regulates the UK's world of broadcasting and telecommunications.

The Water Services Regulation Authority (OFWAT) regulates the water and sewage industries in England and Wales. In Scotland, this role is performed by the Water Industry Commission for Scotland.

The Office of Gas and Electricity Markets (OFGEM) regulates electricity and natural gas providers.

The Office of Rail Regulation (ORR) oversees economics and safety for the railway industry. When the railways were privatized in the 1990s, the powers that be realized the shortcomings of their existing formula for naming such regulatory bodies. In hindsight, "OFRAIL" would have been taken as prophetic, given all the problems the privatized rail system has experienced.

TOP BUSINESS SCHOOLS

Business schools are a relatively new phenomenon in the UK. Though they have been a presence in the US for a long time—Harvard Business School was founded in 1908—British academia has long been resistant. The blatant mixture of education and commerce was considered distasteful, and people wondered if business studies really qualified as an academic subject. When Oxford University first proposed establishing a business school, five hundred dons (teachers) came out to protest. Money usually has its way, however, and today there are a growing number of world-class business schools in the UK, generally offering one-year MBA programs. The *Financial Times* annually lists the world's top business schools; among the most notable are the London Business School, the Judge Business School at the University of Cambridge, and the Saïd Business School at the University of Oxford.

BUSINESS FAQS

What's the "eurozone"?
It's the collective group of countries in the European Union that have adopted the euro as their currency. Since the UK, though a member of the European Union, has not adopted the euro, it is not in the eurozone.

Which are the biggest companies in the UK?
Some of the largest publicly held companies in the UK include BP (oil and gas), HSBC Holdings (banks), Vodafone Group (telecommunications), and Rio Tinto (mining). The FTSE 100 is the *Financial Times* Stock Exchange index of the 100 most highly capitalized companies

traded on the London Stock Exchange. Some of the largest privately held companies include Ineos Group (chemical manufacturer), John Lewis Partnership (retailer), and Virgin Atlantic (airline).

What's a "national insurance number"?

In the UK, a person's national insurance number is similar to a Social Security number in the US and is used by employers for similar tax-reporting purposes.

THE NHS (NATIONAL HEALTH SERVICE)

Given the ongoing discussions about the health-care system in the US, Americans might be particularly interested in learning more about the NHS, which is essentially a socialized medical system. This means that every resident in the UK is covered and is treated at the government's expense. The NHS was established in 1946 and is funded through taxes.

It's possible to see doctors privately and to have private health insurance. One of the main differences between the NHS and private care is that hospitalized NHS patients stay in large wards, where someone with a minor ailment might be in a bed next to someone who is dying. With private care you can avoid the wards and get a more, well, private situation. Also, there are typically longer waits to see NHS doctors than when paying to see a doctor privately.

IN AN EMERGENCY

999 in the UK = 911 in the US

EDUCATION

There are few things as entwined with class, status, and snobbism in the UK as education. Where someone was educated traditionally marks them for life.

Full-time education is mandatory for all children in the UK between ages five and sixteen. At the end of the school year during which a student turns sixteen, they are free to leave—those who do so at this point are referred to as "school-leavers." The government plans to raise the school-leaving age to eighteen starting in 2013, largely in an effort to produce a better-trained workforce and address the persistent 10 percent of sixteen- to eighteen-year-old NEETs (Not in education, employment, or training).

THE STATE SYSTEM: GRAMMAR SCHOOLS, COMPS, AND SECONDARY MODERNS

From the 1940s until the 1970s, all children in the Welsh, English, and Northern Irish state education system took the eleven-plus exam at approximately age eleven. Depending on their exam results—there was no official pass or fail—students entered a grammar school, a technical school, or a secondary modern. Grammar schools were the most prestigious, taking roughly the top quarter of children. Technical schools, or "techs," were few and far between but intended for those who showed an aptitude for science and technical subjects. Secondary moderns took the ungifted majority. Children who made it into the grammar schools received a first-rate learning experience and an open road to a professional career. The other branches were left to wither, providing the majority of children with a substandard education. Opposition to the system came from both ends of the spectrum: the working-class opposed a system that created an elite at the expense of the majority; the middle-class opposed it once they realized the grammar schools weren't reserving spaces for their children.

Under the Labour government of the mid-1970s, the eleven-plus exams and the selective system were phased out, and the schools of the tripartite system were reinvented as comprehensives, so-called because they were intended to provide a comprehensive education for all. Though grammar schools have hung on in some regions, nowadays about 90 percent of children attend comprehensives, or "comps," as they're abbreviated. The grammar schools that do remain trounce the comprehensives in exam results.

In Scotland, the education system is slightly different than in the rest of the UK. Besides actually calling high school "high school," schools in Scotland have their own curriculum and qualification systems.

THE PRIVATE SYSTEM:
PUTTING THE "PRIVATE" IN PUBLIC SCHOOLS

When they reach the tender age of eight years old, traditionally the sons of the upper-classes are shipped out to boarding school in the country. Daughters are sometimes packed off, too, but usually that occurs a few years later. These preparatory schools, or "prep schools" as they are called, ready children for secondary school. Children attend prep school, whether they are boarding or day students, generally from the age of eight to thirteen. At thirteen, they take (or, in British parlance, they "sit") the common entrance exams, which are used by independent secondary schools, sometimes called colleges, to determine admission (and scholarships, often called "bursaries").

After prep school, the next stop for affluent teens is public school, a type of secondary school. It should be said right off the bat that "public school" is a complete misnomer. There is nothing public about them: For boarders, fees can run over £20,000 a year. The term derives from the fact that the schools were public—open to anyone who could pay the fees—in contrast to the private tutors hired by some families. Of course, the term "public school" is now synonymous with posh and privileged. That students at Eton still wear tails to class doesn't do much to dispel this image. Most of the top public schools were single-sex until fairly recently; many are now coed.

In the past, the Labour Party always made a great fuss about abolishing the public schools, but that sort of thing is not heard much anymore. After all, Labour prime minister Tony Blair went to the exclusive Scottish public school Fettes. Today, most griping is targeted at the schools' use of merit rather than means to determine scholarships. Top schools like Eton spend only a few percent of their revenue on needs-based scholarships, a tiny sum when compared with the top American prep schools.

	US	UK
"Prep School"	Ages fourteen to eighteen*	Ages eight to thirteen
"College"	Ages eighteen to twenty-two	Ages fourteen to eighteen

*Ages are approximate.

SOME PROMINENT PUBLIC SCHOOLS

Day Schools for Boys

Westminster, London.
Alumni: Sir John Gielgud (actor), Lord Lloyd Webber (aka Andrew Lloyd Webber, composer).

St. Paul's School, London.
Alumni: Oliver Sacks (neurologist and writer), Sir Isaiah Berlin (philosopher).

Boarding Schools for Boys

Eton College, Windsor, Berkshire (England).
Alumni (called "Old Etonians"): Princes William and Harry (royals), Boris Johnson (mayor of London), David Cameron (Conservative Party leader), Hugh Laurie (actor), Ian Fleming (novelist), James Bond (fictional spy, expelled and went to Fettes; see below).

Harrow School, Harrow-on-the-Hill, Middlesex (England).
Alumni (called "Old Harrovians"): Richard Curtis (screenwriter), James Blunt (musician), Winston Churchill (former prime minister).

Winchester College, Winchester, Hampshire (England).
Alumni (called "Old Wykehamists"): Arnold Toynbee (historian), Kenneth Clark (art historian and TV host), Anthony Beevor (historian).

Day Schools for Girls

St. Paul's Girls' School, London.
Alumni (called "Old Paulinas"): Natasha Richardson (actor), Emma Tennant (novelist).

Frances Holland School, London. This school has two branches, both in London.
Alumni: Joan Collins (actor), Jackie Collins (author), Jemima Khan (socialite).

Godolphin and Latymer School, London.
Alumni (called "Old Dolphins"): Kate Beckinsale (actor), Nigella Lawson (lifestyle guru).

Boarding Schools for Girls

Benenden School, Cranbrook, Kent (England).
Alumni: Princess Anne (royal), Fiona Shackleton (England's top divorce lawyer), Rachel Weisz (actor).

Cheltenham Ladies' College, Cheltenham, Gloucestershire (England).
Alumni: Fiona Mactaggart (MP), Kristin Scott Thomas (actor).

Coed Boarding Schools

Bedales School, Petersfield, Hampshire (England). Famously progressive.
Alumni: Daniel Day-Lewis (actor), Viscount Linley (royal), Minnie
Driver (actor), Sophie Dahl (model and author), Lily Allen (musician).

Fettes College, Edinburgh (Scotland).
Alumni: Tony Blair (former prime minister), Tilda Swinton (actor),
James Bond (fictional spy).

Gordonstoun School, Elgin, Moray (Scotland).
Alumni: Prince Philip (royal), Prince Charles (royal), India Hicks (designer, author, model).

EXAMS

GCSEs (Formerly Known as O Levels)

The yardsticks of adolescence, standardized examinations feature
largely in British education. Exams in the UK are much more important in determining grades than in the US. Between the ages of roughly
six and sixteen, children in the state system sit national curriculum
tests, the last of which are the GCSEs (General Certificate of Secondary Education). Formerly known as the O levels (*O* for "ordinary"), the
GCSEs or their Scottish equivalent, Standard Grades, are taken by virtually every pupil in the British educational system, whether they attend public school or a comprehensive school. Exams are taken in a
number of subjects; how many depend on the student's aptitude and
ambition, though just about everyone takes at least English, science,
and math. For those who leave school following their exams, government figures paint an unpleasant picture of unemployment and poverty
for those with less than five GCSEs, while those with more tend to
have an easier time of it (though there are exceptions to this rule:
Princess Diana failed all of her O levels). Most students take eight or
nine GCSEs; high achievers take up to twelve. There are about a hun-

dred subjects students can take GCSEs in, from food technology to nautical studies. Grades range from A* through G, and finally U, for "unclassified," that is, fail. Broadly speaking, in Britain the numerical grading curve is somewhat different than in the US, with 50 percent traditionally being a passing grade and 70 percent or thereabouts an A, rather than the American 90 percent.

A Levels

Those who do well on their GCSEs and have hopes of attending university will stick around at secondary school for another two years. For these last two years, they will specifically study the courses they've selected to sit A levels in (*A* for "advanced"). Most universities will require three A levels. It is at this point that British students begin the path of hyper-specialization that differentiates the country's higher educational system from the American liberal arts model. The subjects students choose for their A levels can very well determine their future university subjects and subsequent career fields. The closest things in American high schools are advanced placement courses.

There is talk about changing the system. Some critics say it heavily favors those coming from public schools, which have the resources to provide the in-depth expertise A levels require; others say that, in fact, grade inflation is making the results meaningless: twenty-five years ago, only 12 percent of A-level candidates received an A grade, whereas today about 25 percent do, and no one is claiming that the educational system today is twice as good as it was a quarter century ago. (This was a contributing factor to why the A* grade was instituted.) A small but increasing number of schools are opting out of the system, believing it leaves students too narrowly focused too young, and are instead participating in the international baccalaureate (IB) program, based on the broader French system. The government has also made noises about trying to replace A levels with less specialized "diplomas." Top-flight state schools are not interested, however, in replacing their successful A-level university preparatory programs in fields such as history, Latin, and math with training for diplomas in subjects such as "society, health, and development" and "construction and the built environment."

Scotland has a slightly different system. Secondary education there is not so specialized. Rather, students study a broader range of subjects in which they sit highers and advanced highers exams.

UNIVERSITY

The British university experience is very different from the American. Sure, the students drink too much, pull all-nighters before exams, and are perpetually broke, but the similarities end not far from there. Take university admissions: In Britain, candidates for university will declare what subject they want to "read," interview at a couple of universities, and then receive conditional "offers" provided their A-level grades meet requirements. Oxford and Cambridge, collectively referred to as "Oxbridge," will generally make offers contingent on A-level results of "AAA," or A's in three A-level exams (though the new grade A* is being added to supersede an A). The interviewers are looking for academic prowess; they don't much care that the student was captain of the track team and spent their weekends helping old ladies cross the street. Along these lines, sports are pretty inconsequential at the university level. No TV contracts, seven-figure-salaried coaches, and mega-stadiums here, just friendly extramural clubs.

Academically, the biggest difference is the level of specialization. A freshman, or "fresher" in British parlance, who embarks on an English literature degree will study nothing but English literature for the three years of their undergraduate career (four years in Scotland). As a result, British graduates will have a base of knowledge in their subject comparable to an American with a master's degree, though an American college graduate from a comparable institution will have a broader foundation.

With the British system's emphasis on exams there is not really anything like the US grade point average. Students take quizzes and write essays, but these generally don't count toward their final grades. While it varies from course to course, students will take Part 1 exams at the end of their second year, which count toward, but are not decisive in determining, the rank of their final degree. In the final term of their university careers, students will submit a dissertation and sit exams on their final year of courses, and these grades are the ones that count heaviest in determining the quality of degree received.

Those who excel will receive a first-class degree, called a "first"; next is an upper-second-class degree, called a "two-one"; then comes the lower-second-class degree, or "two-two," sometimes affectionately known as a "Desmond" in a rhyming slang reference to Nobel laureate Desmond Tutu; at the bottom are third-class degrees or ordinary degrees; anything below that is a failure for which no degree is awarded.

As with secondary education, Scotland is a little less narrow in its focus. There, university courses generally run four years instead of three. The first two include studies ranging a little beyond just the subject that the student is reading. Due to the extra year, some Scottish universities award a master's degree to graduates who excel at their exams.

Twenty years ago, less than 20 percent of British students graduated from schools of higher education, which includes both universities and the less prestigious polytechnics, which have since been absorbed into the university system. Back then, for those lucky enough to attend, education was free, and students received both housing grants and living stipends from the government. Nowadays, 35 percent of young people graduate from university, a figure higher than even the US, but the free ride is gone. All but the poorest students have to pay fees—a maximum of £3,145 (about $5,000) for the 2008–9 academic year, so it's still cheap compared to US universities—as well as housing and living expenses. (For students attending British universities from outside the European Union, fees run from £10,500 to £23,500, depending on the course. That's approximately $16,500 to $37,000 at late 2008 conversion rates.)

Despite the expense, attending university is becoming an increasingly important requirement to succeed in both the UK and global economies. More jobs than ever advertise now for "graduates." Fortunately, even without the enormous endowments and alumni generosity of American universities, Britain's institutions of higher education have managed to retain their world-class reputations.

EDUCATION FAQS

What's a "gap year"?
Students will sometimes opt to take a year off before starting university. They might travel or enroll in a year-long study program. While some American students do this, it's more common in the UK.

What are the UK equivalents of freshman, sophomore, junior, and senior?
First-year university students are called "freshers." From there a student becomes a "second year" then a "third year" then, in Scotland where university goes for four years, a "fourth year."

What's the difference between a lecturer, senior reader, and professor?
While most university teachers in the US are generally referred to as "professor," in the UK there is a more specific hierarchy. They begin as lecturers then progress to senior readers and professors.

How are Americans studying in the UK viewed by students there, and how are their credits transferred?
Generally speaking, British students have no animosity toward Americans studying abroad. However, American students must make the effort to get to know their British classmates. Suggestions for doing this include dating a Brit and finding programs where Americans and Brits are integrated in housing arrangements and classes. As for credits, American universities usually have study-abroad programs from which they accept credits, often on a pass-fail basis.

MARKS & SPENCER

There are few institutions that unite the British regardless of class, geography, or wealth, but one is the department store Marks & Spencer, affectionately known as "Marks and Sparks" or even just "M&S." Be they an earl or unemployed, there's a fine chance that any Brit you meet will be wearing underwear, if not more, from the store. Founded by Michael Marks, one of the hundreds of thousands of Polish and Russian Jewish immigrants to Britain in the second half of the nineteenth century, Marks & Spencer has more than five hundred stores in the UK. Marks started with a market stall in the northern city of Leeds, hit upon the slogan "Don't ask the price—it's a penny," and took on a partner, Thomas Spencer, to found the company in 1894. Within a decade they had forty-plus shops. Today things cost a little more than a penny, but Marks and Sparks remains a staple for quality and value in food and clothing.

THE METRIC SYSTEM

You'd think the land that invented the foot, the inch, and the pound would be able to fend off the metric system. Alas, that wasn't in the cards. This can get a little confusing. Gas, or "petrol," is sold in liters, which is great since it makes it seem so cheap. It's only when you remember that there are about four liters to a gallon (a liter is a little over a quart) that you begin to realize just how expensive it is.

In the supermarket aisles, a few commonly found package sizes and their rough equivalents:

62 grams = about one-eighth pound
100 grams = between one-fifth pound and one-quarter pound
250 grams = just over one-half pound
500 grams = 1.1 pounds
1 kilogram = 2.2 pounds

For distances, miles are still frequently given, but you can't depend on it. Remember the old rule of thumb: eight kilometers is five miles.

With the weather, Fahrenheit is completely out the window. There aren't many solid benchmarks between Fahrenheit and Celsius, but these few will help:

- Water freezes at 32°F and 0°C.
- 50°F is 10°C.
- 61°F is 16°C.
- 68°F is 20°C.
- 77°F is 25°C.
- 86°F is 30°C.

You won't need to know any comparisons beyond this, as the temperature in the UK will rarely go higher.

> People are weighed in stone.
> One stone = Fourteen pounds

LAW AND ORDER

SCOTLAND YARD

Scotland Yard is the headquarters of London's Metropolitan Police and, deceptively enough, it's not actually in Scotland. The original headquarters were in the Whitehall area of London (see page 134). The building had an entrance that opened onto Great Scotland Yard, named for the medieval palace at the site where Scottish royalty stayed when visiting—hence the name "Scotland Yard."

To this day, the Metropolitan Police are often referred to as "Scotland Yard." To complicate matters, however, the headquarters are no longer located in Scotland Yard but are in Westminster and called "New Scotland Yard."

The Metropolitan Police oversees all of greater London except for the City of London, which has its own police force. In 1829, Home Secretary Sir Robert Peel introduced an act in Parliament that resulted in the creation of this separate force; it is for Sir Robert that these police officers are nicknamed "bobbies."

ASBO

ASBO, pronounced "az-bow," stands for anti-social behavior order. They've been around since 1999 and are issued to people who have outdone themselves in being obnoxious or menacing to their communities. An ASBO is supposed to keep someone from going to a certain place or engaging in a certain activity, sort of like a restraining order. In case you're wondering about the type of behavior it takes to get an ASBO, here are some examples:

A thirty-year-old woman, as reported by the BBC, was given an ASBO for repeatedly playing the hit single "Amarillo" by Tony Christie and Peter Kay at high volume.

In 2007, a courtroom heard the story of an eighty-one-year-old woman who reportedly disregarded her ASBO and continued abusing a family in her neighborhood, calling the wife a prostitute and hitting her with a stick; posting photographs of the family's house with the label "scum"; and notifying their thirteen-year-old daughter that she was a witch and intended to cast a spell over the family. Despite her age, "the ASBO granny," as the *Daily Mail* tagged her, received a six-month prison sentence.

In March 2008, a thirty-six-year-old woman was given an ASBO after calling 999 (which is like 911 in the US) more than one hundred times while drunk to ask for a ride home. Under her ASBO this woman can call 999 only in a real emergency, is now banned from about seventy drinking establishments, and cannot be drunk in public.

WHAT'S THE DIFFERENCE BETWEEN
A BARRISTER AND A SOLICITOR?

The legal profession in Britain is split into two branches: solicitors and barristers (called "advocates" in Scotland). When someone needs legal help, they employ a solicitor. Like lawyers in the US, solicitors generally work for law firms, government agencies, or corporations and will often specialize in various types of law, such as criminal, corporate, and so on.

Barristers are hired by solicitors to offer specialist advice and to present cases in court prepared by the solicitors (though solicitors can and will argue cases themselves in lower courts, with some also permitted to do so in the higher courts). Barristers are by and large self-employed professionals, banded together in offices called "chambers." A QC (queen's counsel) is a senior barrister. When there is a king, this title will immediately change to KC (king's counsel).

Solicitors share profits with other partners of the firm, while barristers generally pay a percentage of what they earn to cover the chamber's expenses and then keep the rest themselves. While in court, barristers and judges both traditionally wear the gowns and the white horsehair wigs we are familiar with from the movies, though nowadays this is rare for civil cases. For criminal cases, however, wigs and gowns continue to have strong support and are likely to remain for some time.

FAMOUS CRIMINALS OF THE UK

The **Kray twins**, Reggie and Ronnie, are perhaps the most notorious modern criminals in the UK. From the East End of London they built an organized crime empire in the 1950s and 1960s, replete with (alleged) armed robbery, extortion, drug dealing, and murder. In 1969, at the age of thirty-five, they were convicted of one murder each and sentenced to life imprisonment. Ronnie and Reggie led high-profile lives until going to jail. Ronnie died in 1995 and Reggie in 2000.

One of Britain's most spectacular crimes, the **Great Train Robbery** took place on the Glasgow-to-London mail train on August 8, 1963. In a well-coordinated ambush, about fifteen robbers stopped the train outside of London and stole approximately £2,600,000 in cash. The engineer received serious blows to his head, but no one else was injured. A record £260,000 reward for information was offered the next day. The robbers fled to a farmhouse in Buckinghamshire, where police later found fingerprints and started making arrests. One of the robbers arrested, **Ronnie Biggs,** was sentenced to thirty years in jail but escaped from Wandsworth prison in 1965 and fled the country. He ended up in Brazil, where he eluded extradition for decades. He voluntarily returned to the UK for medical treatment in 2001 and was promptly arrested. While living in Brazil, Ronnie Biggs wrote his memoir and even recorded a song, "No One Is Innocent," with the Sex Pistols, who traveled to South America to meet him. Buster Edwards, another member of the gang, was further punished after fifteen years in jail by having Phil Collins play him in the 1988 movie *Buster.*

Myra Hindley and her boyfriend **Ian Brady** were convicted in 1966 of a series of grisly murders. Hindley was found guilty of murdering two teenagers and Brady of murdering three—all involving torture and sexual abuse. Known as the "Moors Murderers," the duo spent decades in jail. Hindley died in 2002 of a chest infection, and Brady is still in jail as of 2009, though he is petitioning to be allowed to starve to death. Hindley maintained that Brady had threatened her and her family if she didn't participate in the murders. It was later reported that the two killed other victims as well.

Dr. Harold Shipman was a respected member of the community in Manchester—that is, until he was convicted in 2000 for murdering fifteen of his patients. He is suspected of killing more than two hundred others over the course of his career. Most of his victims were elderly women to whom he gave lethal injections of heroin. He was caught when he was accused of forging the will of a patient who had died at his office. Sentenced to life in prison, he hanged himself in his cell in 2004.

The **Yorkshire Ripper,** aka Peter Sutcliffe, was a truck driver who in 1981 was jailed for life after being convicted of thirteen counts of murder and seven counts of attempted murder. His victims were largely prostitutes whom he beat to death in the years between 1976 and 1981. A few years later, his wife, Sonia Sutcliffe, sued the satirical political magazine *Private Eye* for libel when the magazine said she had sold her story to the *Daily Mail* shortly after her husband was charged. She won an astounding £600,000 in damages, which was later reduced to £60,000 upon appeal.

Fred and Rosemary West were serial killers prone to raping, torturing, and killing young girls, many of whom they buried under their house in Gloucester. In 1994, they were charged with murder after an investigation into the disappearance of their sixteen-year-old daughter. Ultimately Rosemary West was charged with ten murders and Fred West with twelve. Their victims included their own daughter, Fred's daughter from a previous marriage, and Fred's pregnant lover. Fred West killed himself in jail while waiting for trial, and Rosemary West was sentenced to life imprisonment in 1995. She appealed the conviction unsuccessfully.

BIG BROTHER IS WATCHING

When you walk down the street, ride on the bus, or drive your car on the motorway in the UK, remember to smile and look your best because, without a doubt, you're on candid camera. According to a report by the BBC in 2007, there are 4.2 million cameras in the UK, and the average person is filmed on CCTV (closed caption television) about three hundred times per day.

Billions of dollars were spent on these cameras in an effort to reduce crime, though whether they're working is a matter of debate. Even if the crime rate hasn't dropped, however, images from CCTV have been used in solving crimes. The problem has been sorting through the immense volume of information generated by the cameras and using it effectively, though recently the police have introduced software programs to do this.

Cameras along the road will also photograph your license plate if you're speeding or breaking other traffic rules. This has led to an industry of tricks and gadgets, from fake plates to a reflective coating that blacks out in pictures, designed to help motorists avoid tickets.

Privacy activists argue that the information from CCTV cameras can be misused and that people shouldn't be filmed going about their everyday lives. Those in favor of the widespread use of CCTV argue that it can reduce crime and will save money down the road.

DEATH PENALTY

The abolition of the death penalty for murder was permanently enacted by Parliament in 1969. There were still some crimes, though, such as treason, for which the death penalty could be sought. In 1999, the UK ratified Protocol 6 of the European Convention on Human Rights, which is a human rights treaty committing a country to the permanent and complete abolition of the death penalty. This treaty has been ratified by all EU member states.

FAMOUS RIOTS

Notting Hill Riots, 1958

In the summer of 1958, tensions in London's North Kensington neighborhood of Notting Hill were mounting. Many Caribbean immigrants had recently moved into the area, which created competition for jobs and housing with the white working-class families who already lived there. It came to a head at the end of August when for five days, into early September, riots raged between the West Indians and the teddy boys, young, white, rock and roll–listening greasers.

At the time, police downplayed any racial motivation for the riots, but it later surfaced that white gangs deliberately targeted black immigrants. This was at the same time racial violence was churning in the southern US, and many in Britain were surprised to see this sort of violence in their own country.

The year following the riots, a West Indian carnival in Notting Hill was established to restore peace and harmony. However, during the carnival in 1976, violence erupted once again in Notting Hill—the Clash's Joe Strummer and Paul Simonon were caught up in the ruckus, which later inspired the 1977 song "White Riot."

The Bogside Riots, Northern Ireland, 1969

After a long buildup of tension between Catholics and Protestants in the Northern Irish city of Londonderry (the Catholics call it Derry), three days of rioting, known as the "Battle of the Bogside," erupted in August 1969. Catholics, who were under attack from the Protestants, had been staging civil rights protests. When violence broke out, they barricaded the primarily Protestant Royal Ulster Constabulary (RUC) police force from the Catholic Bogside neighborhood.

The British army was called in to protect the Catholics, though the Catholics soon saw the army as an occupying force. The army remained on the streets of Northern Ireland for more than thirty years.

Brixton, 1981

Tensions were high in this high-crime, low-employment neighborhood in south London. Young black men felt they weren't being treated fairly by the police, who had instituted "Operation Swamp," an edict allowing plainclothes police to stop and search people based only on suspicion they might commit a crime. One night in April, police stopped to help a young black man who had been stabbed. A hostile crowd approached, thinking the man was being arrested, and the trouble began. When another young man was stopped and searched the following day, it triggered a full-fledged battle between police and neighborhood residents. Rioting lasted for three days and resulted in more than three hundred injuries, as well as the looting and burning of local stores and residences.

Order was restored, but the underlying antagonism remained. In 1985, there were more riots in Brixton after a police officer accidentally shot a woman during a raid.

REAL ESTATE TRANSACTIONS

Real estate transactions in the UK have some critical differences from those in the US. Below are some helpful things to know.

Freehold versus Leasehold

A freehold property is one that you own completely. A leasehold property means you own the property for as long as a lease indicates; it could be 60 years or 100 years or even 999 years. In this case, the property is owned by the freeholder, who grants you the right to live there for as long as the lease is valid. Most leasehold sales are for apartments; houses are more likely to be freehold. Under laws passed in the 1990s to break up the large leasehold estates of London, leaseholders can force owners to sell them the freehold.

Weekly versus Monthly Rentals

If you're perusing flats for rent in the window of a real estate agent's office and think "Wow, things aren't as expensive in the UK as people say," maybe you missed the part on the flyer that says "per week." It's common for UK rents to be charged on a weekly basis, instead of a monthly one.

REAL ESTATE TERMINOLOGY

Bedsit. A combined bedroom and sitting room, usually with a kitchenette.

Council house. Public housing provided by government at low subsidized rents. The Right to Buy scheme gives council tenants the right to buy the property at a discount.

Estate. Housing project.

Mansion block. Upmarket block of older apartments.

Mod cons. Short for "modern conveniences." Things like dishwashers, washing machines, and dryers are mod cons. Real estate listings will say "all mod cons."

Purpose-built. A modern apartment building.

To let. Instead of "to rent" you will see "to let" signs, which mean the same thing.

Tower block. High-rise apartment building, typically built post-WWII.

FACT OR FICTION?

Brits love the sun.
Fact. Wouldn't you if it rained half the year at home? The beaches of the Mediterranean are littered with lumpen pale British bodies.

Brits love their animals more than their children.
Fact. The Brits are famously animal obsessive. Annual donations to the national animal charity the RSPCA (Royal Society for the Prevention of Cruelty to Animals) are slightly higher than those to the NSPCC (National Society for the Prevention of Cruelty to Children).

A good Englishman would never go into debt.
Fiction. The UK has one of the highest rates of personal debt in the developed world.

The English are loved and admired in Europe.
Fiction. The charm of their drunken rampages wore off centuries ago.

*The British drive on the left side of the road because back in the Middle Ages it
was better, as a right-handed person, to face potentially unfriendly oncoming traffic from the side of your body in which you held your sword.*

Fact. The Middle Ages were a rough time during which everyone traveled on the left side of the road, a practice confirmed by papal edict.
Today, the British, the Japanese, and a number of Commonwealth
countries retain this practice. The harder question is why Americans
and others drive on the right. The French appear to have been the first
to mandate keeping to the right side of the road in their revolutionary
zeal to upend old ways. For Americans, it was allegedly more practical:
Right-handed coach and wagon drivers sat on the left side of their
wagon seats, held their reins in the center, and thus had better visibil-
ity by keeping to the right side of the road. Of course, none of this ex-
plains why British boats, unlike automobiles, keep to the right.

*A major pilgrimage destination for people of the UK is the Diana and Dodi
memorial at Harrods. Most English, Scottish, Welsh, and Northern Irish people
try to get there at least once a year to pay their respects.*

Fiction. Though the memorial gets plenty of visitors, many are from other
countries and not everyone in the UK is going to want to hear about your
visit to the memorial and how much it meant to you. The memorial, by
the way, is in the basement at Harrods, near the Egyptian stairs.

Wormwood Scrubs is a fictional prison in the Harry Potter series of books.

Fiction. It is a real prison in west London. Other amusingly named
British prisons include Strangeways in Manchester and the now-closed
Maze in Northern Ireland.

*The identity of Jack the Ripper is one of the great unsolved mysteries. Despite
elaborate efforts, the serial killer was never found.*

Fact. In 1888, at least five prostitutes were found brutally murdered in
London's East End. Police went to great lengths to catch the killer but
never did. Many books filled with speculation about the killer's identity have been written.

ACKNOWLEDGMENTS

We are enormously grateful to so many people for their help with this book. Or, rather, we should say we're well chuffed to have had so many friends help us suss this out. Without the sparks of genius, brainstorming, expertise, and support from the following people, *Britannia in Brief* would be just another idea sitting on some shelf gathering dust: Wyndham Lewis, Liz Doyle Carey, Lily Malcom, Alex Hutton, Jenny Tooze, Mark Brookes, Hannah Swett, Mary Langford, Bill and Pippa James, Sarah and Gerard Griffin, Courtenay Palmer, Tom Mullins, and Jasmin Rubero helped us turn a concept into a book, as well as shored up our knowledge on such things as the particulars of cricket, football icons, snooker, libel laws, and celebrity culture, to name just a few.

Of course, our families gave us lots ideas and encouragement. Tommy Mullins, Brewer Schoeller, and David and Pam Banker were, as always, enthusiastic supporters.

Last but certainly not least, it has been a pleasure to work with Jillian Quint, the team at Random House, and our agent, Claudia Cross. Their brilliant thoughts and guidance have shaped this book into just what we imagined it would be.

UK ACRONYMS

A & E. Accident and Emergency Department, aka emergency room.

ASA. Advertising Standards Authority.

ASBO. Anti-social behavior order (see page 206).

BAFTA. British Academy of Film and Television Arts (see page 125).

BNP. British National Party (see page 141).

BUPA. The British United Provident Association. A large private health insurance company.

DUP. Democrat Unionist Party (Northern Ireland, see page 141).

FSA. Financial Services Authority.

GBH. Grievous bodily harm. You'll read about people being charged by the police with "GBH."

GCSE. General Certificate of Secondary Education.

GLC. Greater London Council.

HM. His or Her Majesty.

HMNB. His or Her Majesty's Naval Base. There are three of these—HMNB Portsmouth, HMNB Clyde, and HMNB Devonport—and they are the Royal Navy's operating bases. HMNB Devonport, also known as HMS Drake, is the largest naval base in Western Europe.

HMRC. Her Majesty's Revenue and Customs, like the Internal Revenue Service.

HMS. Her Majesty's Service—the civil service.

HMS. His or Her Majesty's Ship, Submarine, or Station of the Royal Navy. This last usage can be confusing. HMS Sultan, for example, is actually the navy's completely land-based school of engineering, and yet there was also a nineteenth-century ironclad battleship of the same name.

IRA. Irish Republican Army (see page 141).

ISA. Individual Savings Account.

LSE. London Stock Exchange (see page 190).

MCC. Marylebone Cricket Club (see page 87).

MEP. Member of European Union Parliament (based in Brussels).

MOD. Ministry of Defense.

MP. Member of Parliament (meaning British parliament).

MSP. Member of the Scottish parliament.

NCO. Noncommissioned officer.

NEET. Not in education, employment, or training (see page 195).

NHS. National Health Service (see page 194).

NSPCC. National Society for the Prevention of Cruelty to Children.

OAP. Old-age pensioner.

OFT. Office of Fair Trading.

ORR. Office of Rail Regulation.

PLC. Public limited company, similar to the US "Corp."

QUANGO. Quasi-Autonomous Nongovernmental Organization.

RAF. Royal Air Force.

RN. Royal Navy.

RNLI. Royal National Lifeboat Institution.

RSPCA. Royal Society for the Prevention of Cruelty to Animals.

SAS. Special Air Service.

SDLP. Social Democrat and Labour Party (Northern Ireland, see page 141).

SFO. Serious Fraud Office.

SIS. Secret Intelligence Service.

SNP. Scottish National Party (see page 139).

TA. Territorial army. Britain's reserve military force, composed of part-time soldiers available in case of war.

TUC. Trades Union Congress, the national federation of trade unions.

UB40. Not just the name of a pop band, but the Unemployment Benefit Form 40 that people (including UB40 band members) filled out to receive the dole. The form doesn't exist anymore, though the term "UB40" might still be used to mean unemployment claims.

UUP. Ulster Unionist Party (Northern Ireland, see page 141).

VC. Victoria Cross, Britain's highest military medal.

WAG. Wives and girlfriends (of footballers, see page 83).

GLOSSARY

Anorak. A lightweight parka. The word is also used as a synonym for "nerd" or "geek."

Baggage. Luggage.

Bog. Bathroom ("bog roll" means "toilet paper").

Chelsea tractor. SUV.

Chemist. Pharmacy.

Chuffed. Happy.

Daft. Stupid.

Dinner jacket. Black tie. (Tuxedo is considered a very naff word.)

Faff. To procrastinate or spend time doing nothing.

Fag. A cigarette.

High street. Main street. "High street stores" is the term for big national stores or stores found in every town. The Gap would be a high street store.

Highway code. Rules of the road.

Hogmanay. New Year's Eve celebration in Scotland.

Holiday. Vacation.

Hoover. Vacuum.

Inland Revenue. Tax office, like the IRS.

Jumper. Sweater.

Loo. Bathroom.

Marks and Sparks. The department store Marks & Spencer.

Naff. Tasteless.

Noughts and Crosses. Tic Tac Toe.

Oxbridge. Oxford and Cambridge universities collectively.

Pants. Underwear.

Plimsoll. Sneaker.

Porridge. A prison sentence. "Doing porridge" is serving time.

Punter. Customer.

Queue. Line.

Rubbish bin (or "bin"). Garbage can.

Sectioned. Involuntarily incarcerated, such as "sectioned under the Mental Health Act."

Sellotape. Sticky tape.

Skint. Broke.

Stone. Fourteen pounds, used for a person's weight.

Swat or **Swot.** To study. To call someone "a swat" is to call them a nerd.

Ta. Thanks.

Tab. Northern term for cigarette.

Tea towel. Dish towel.

Teddy Boy. A 1950s rock 'n roll subculture with a distinctive Edwardian-inspired fashion sense.

Toff. Upper-class, public (that is, private) school twit.

Tombola. Raffle.

Totty. Hottie.

Trainers. Sneakers.

Vest. Tank top; undershirt.

Waistcoat. A man's sleeveless, collarless vest worn under a jacket.

Washing powder. Laundry detergent.

Washing up liquid. Dish soap.

Wellies. Wellington boots, which are rubber knee-high boots.

Wide boy. A wheeler-and-dealer type; someone who spreads himself wide.

Wobbler. Fit; to throw a wobbler is to throw a fit.

Wonga. Money.

Yardie. Jamaican gangster.

THE *BRITANNIA IN BRIEF* QUIZ

1. The Troubles were:
   a. The conflict in Northern Ireland that started in the late 1960s.
   b. One of the bestselling British punk bands.
   c. An award-winning television sitcom on the BBC in the 1970s.

2. If you are attending a wedding in Scotland, wearing a kilt is:
   a. A great idea whether you're Scottish or not.
   b. Not a great idea unless you have very close ties to Scotland.
   c. Mandatory.

3. True or False: The UK is a member of the European Union.

4. True or False: England was occupied by the Romans about two thousand years ago.

5. True or False: The Falklands War was the UK versus Brazil.

6. True or False: A knight is the lowest rank of the peerage.

7. True or False: A duke trumps an earl.

8. Brenda and Phil the Greek are nicknames for:
   a. Victoria and David Beckham.
   b. Queen Elizabeth II and Prince Philip, Duke of Edinburgh.
   c. Tony and Cherie Blair.

9. True or False: *Hello!* magazine is known for its negative stories about celebrities.

10. True or False: Katie Price and Jordan are the same person.

11. Jilly Cooper is:
    a. Lead singer of the girl group Atomic Kitten.
    b. Bestselling author of "bonkbuster" novels.
    c. The current home secretary.

12. True or False: Londonderry and Derry are the same place.

13. Chequers is:
    a. A swank nightclub in London.
    b. The national pastime of Wales.
    c. Like Camp David is for the US president, the official country house for the prime minister.

14. Plaid Cymru is:
    a. A popular clothes designer.
    b. The English national swan society.
    c. The Welsh nationalist political party.

15. True or False: Former London mayor Ken Livingstone is an avid collector of newts.

16. The poll tax was:
    a. Instituted in 1989; individuals were taxed rather than real estate.
    b. Instituted in 1867; registered voters had to pay to vote.
    c. Instituted in 1948; additional income taxes were charged to cover the National Health Service.

17. True or False: The 1966 World Cup was a moment of terrible defeat for the English.

18. True or False: WAG stands for "wives and girlfriends."

19. True or False: A silly mid-off is a field position in cricket.

20. French and Saunders are:
   a. A popular comedic duo who had their own TV show.
   b. The names of two peers involved in a land-use scandal in 1976.
   c. Perhaps the best snooker players of all time.

21. Match the Peel with the profession:
   a. Emma Peel   1. Super-sexy secret agent from the classic 1960s
   b. Robert Peel   TV series *The Avengers.*
   c. John Peel   2. Groundbreaking BBC radio disc jockey.
                       3. Home secretary in the nineteenth century who
                          founded the modern police force.

22. In snooker, the maximum number of points that can be scored on a break is:
   a. 124.
   b. 142.
   c. 147.

23. True or False: Marc Bolan of T. Rex is the father of glam rock.

24. Paul Weller of the Jam and Style Council is known as:
   a. The Modfather.
   b. The Vicar of Vice.
   c. The Grandfather of Punk.

25. True or False: *Blue Peter* is a late-night adults-only television program.

26. True or False: Simon Cowell is a big media mogul in the UK.

27. If someone mentions "Beeb," he or she is referring to:

   a. A beloved character from the soap opera *EastEnders*.

   b. A brand of chocolate sauce.

   c. The BBC (British Broadcasting Corporation).

28. The pub on *Coronation Street* is called:

   a. The Queen Vic.

   b. The Rovers Return.

   c. The Swarthy Knight.

29. Legendary DJ John Peel's favorite song was:

   a. "Pictures of Lily" by the Who.

   b. "Oh, You Pretty Things" by David Bowie.

   c. "Teenage Kicks" by the Undertones.

30. A haggis is:

   a. A small, furry mammal that lives in the Scottish Highlands.

   b. Like a deer, but the males have a more impressive rack.

   c. Boiled lamb organs that are minced and stuffed into a stomach casing.

31. Proper etiquette is to pass the port to the:

   a. Port (that is, the left).

   b. Starboard (that is, the right).

   c. Never pass the port; wait to be served.

32. True or False: A Yorkie bar is advertised as: "It's not for girls!"

33. Branston Pickle is:

   a. A bad situation.

   b. A sweet and tangy condiment.

   c. Too naughty to print.

34. True or False: Always tip the bartender at a pub.

35. Paul McCartney's nickname in the UK is:

   a. Pacca

   b. Macca

   c. Paulio

36. True or False: "Wanker" and "tosser" have more or less the same meaning.

37. True or False: Scotland Yard used to be based in Edinburgh but has recently moved to Dundee.

38. The M25 is a

   a. Bus route that circles London.

   b. Motorway that circles London.

   c. A spy organization.

39. Oxbridge is:

   a. A combination of Oxford and Cambridge, implying students who went to either university. It's as if there were a word "Harvale" for Harvard and Yale collectively.

   b. Where Princess Diana was born.

   c. Where the famed iron bridge is located.

40. The MOT is:

   a. The leading literary publication in the UK.

   b. The Ministry of Transport test, a car inspection.

   c. The Mother of Troubles, a slang expression.

41. True or False: Residents of London living inside the congestion zone are exempt from paying the congestion charge.

42. Guy Fawkes Day celebrates

   a. The foiled Gunpowder Plot.

   b. Gay culture in the UK.

   c. The great civil liberties leader of the 1960s.

43. An ASBO is:
    a. A megamillions lottery ticket.
    b. Slang for an aspirational bohemian.
    c. An anti-social behavior order..

44. True or False: The Clash's song "White Riot" was inspired by violence at the Notting Hill carnival in 1976.

45. An A level is:
    a. A subject-specific test taken to get into university.
    b. A subject-specific test taken to get into high school.
    c. A minor crime, like a misdemeanor.

QUIZ ANSWERS

Score 1 point for each correct answer.

Total score:

45–35 Brilliant!

34–25 Your cultural literacy is Brit-ish.

24–15 Not impressed.

14–0 Pooh. You clearly haven't read *Britannia in Brief.*

1. a (page 14); 2. b (page 55); 3. True (page 5); 4. True (page 6); 5. False:
UK vs. Argentina (page 10); 6. False: Baron is the lowest rank of peer
(page 34); 7. True (page 34); 8. b (page 37); 9. False: *Hello!* is known for its
positive stories on celebrities (page 63); 10. True (page 67); 11. b (page 71);
12. True: Protestants call it Londonderry, and Catholics call it Derry
(page 15); 13. c (page 134); 14. c (page 139); 15. True (page 143); 16. a
(page 147); 17. False: The 1966 World Cup was a moment of great triumph
(page 82); 18. True (page 83); 19. True (page 85); 20. a (page 113); 21. a-1, b-3,
c-2 (page 206, 123); 22. c (page 94); 23. True (page 98); 24. a (page 99);
25. False: *Blue Peter* is a long-running children's show (page 121); 26. True
(page 130); 27. c (page 115); 28. b (page 120); 29. c (page 123); 30. c
(page 156); 31. a (page 151); 32. True (page 154); 33. b (page 155); 34. False: It's
not the custom to leave a tip at the bar of a pub (page 165); 35. b (page 172);
36. True (page 175); 37. False: Scotland Yard is based in London and always has
been (page 225); 38. b (page 183); 39. a (page 201); 40. b (page 183); 41. False:
Residents of the congestion zone get a 90 percent discount on the
congestion charges (page 185); 42. a (page 189); 43. c (page 206); 44. True
(page 211); 45. a (page 200).

INDEX

About the Authors

LESLIE BANKER is the co-author of *The Pocket Decorator* and *The Pocket Renovator*.

WILLIAM MULLINS is a financial software developer and has written freelance pieces for salon.com and *The Boston Book Review*. Before moving to the United States he was an assistant editor at Debrett's publishing in London.